GOD'S MONUMENT TO THE CHRISTIAN.

See page 113.

THROUGH THE EYE TO THE HEART;

OR,

EYE-TEACHING IN THE SUNDAY-SCHOOL.

[*REVISED EDITION.*]

By Rev. W. F. CRAFTS,

Author of "THE COMING MAN IS THE PRESENT CHILD," "TROPHIES OF SONG," "IDEAL SUNDAY-SCHOOL," etc.

WITH AN INTRODUCTION BY J. H. VINCENT, D.D.

"Open thou mine eyes, that I may behold wondrous things out of thy law."

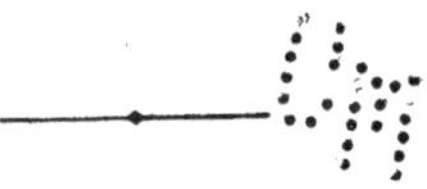

NEW YORK:
NELSON & PHILLIPS.
CINCINNATI:
HITCHCOCK & WALDEN.

TO MY FATHER,

REV. F. A. CRAFTS,

WHO LED ME TO CHRIST BOTH BY WHAT I *HEARD* FROM HIS LIPS, AND WHAT I *SAW* IN HIS LIFE,

This Book is lovingly Dedicated.

INTRODUCTION.

THIS volume on the power and method of "Eye-teaching," which I am requested to "introduce to the Sunday-school public," needs no words of explanation or compliment. Its pages speak for themselves. The book is a defense of a most ancient method of teaching—so old that we cannot recall the time when men who thought and taught at all did not employ it. We find it in Eden, when God gave man his first command ; at Sinai, when Moses taught God's chosen people both law and gospel by complicated and impressive symbols; in Israel, by the Hiddekel, and in Babylon, when holy prophets gave forth burning words from the invisible God; in Galilee and in Judea, when He who "spake as never man spake" taught the thronging multitudes the love and power and sweetness that were to be found in his own divine Gospel. Prophets, priests, apostles, philosophers, reformers, and teachers of all ages and of every nation, have used it. To-day, in the primary school, the academy, college, on the popular rostrum, and in every court of justice, it is continually employed.

This book is more than a defense. It is a guide-book to all the practical details of the art. If the author errs at all it is in the excess of examples which he furnishes. He illustrates the whole field of illustration. One is left in no doubt as to what he means by a principle or a definition. He also exposes many of the mistakes which enthusiasts in chalk have made, reminding the teacher that things thoroughly good may be sadly abused.

Let not those who use "Through the Eye to the Heart" forget that after all it is the SPIRIT, and not alone the truth, that is to reach and regenerate and enrich the heart. The clear apprehension of truth does not necessarily bring the affections and the life into harmony with the truth. For this interior and divine and most essential work we stand in daily need, both as teachers and pupils, of the "Holy Ghost sent down from heaven." For this gift—for this TEACHER who shall "teach us all things"—let us look with the faith that is the "evidence of things not seen." J. H. VINCENT.

NEW YORK, *March*, 1873.

PREFACE TO REVISED EDITION.

THE author's purpose in the theoretical portions of this book is to show that eye-teaching is a legitimate method of teaching, and, also, that it is practicable for all pastors, superintendents, and teachers of average ability; not requiring any unusual ingenuity or artistic talent for its successful use, and as appropriate for the teacher's slate as for the school blackboard.

The exercises will be found to be briet and suggestive rather than elaborate and exhaustive, the desire being to stimulate thought and study rather than take their place. Mrs. Crafts having published "Open Letters to Primary Teachers," in which the subject of illustration in Primary Classes is fully treated, the appendix on that subject from her pen is omitted in this edition.

W. F. C.

CONTENTS.

CONTENTS.

THROUGH THE EYE TO THE HEART.

EYE-TEACHING IN THE SUNDAY-SCHOOL.

THE great object of the Sunday-school is not to organize its members into a picnic club, or a library association, or a singing-school, or a theological institute; not merely to please, or discipline, or teach, as the *end* in view, but by *means* of all these to accomplish its great purpose, TO PRESENT CHRIST TO THE HEART.

Christ is to be the Alpha and Omega, the beginning and the ending, the first and the last, in Sunday-school work. He must be above all, and in all, and through all the exercises.

A little child climbed up in her chair at home to preach to her little brothers and sisters. She turned to the right and said, "Jesus;" then to the front and said, "Jesus;" then to the left and said, "Jesus," and her sermon was ended. So in the Sunday-school we must begin and continue and end with "Jesus."

Though a school can speak at concerts with the tongues of men and of angels, and though its blackboard be always attractive, its superintendent always pleasant, and its numbers large, yet if it only talks *about* Christ instead of *talking Christ*, if it only *pleases* without *saving* its scholars, all its machinery and outward success are but as "sounding brass and a tinkling cymbal." Like one of the English light-houses, the Sunday-school should have the double inscription, "*To give light, to save life.*" A boy with a Testament was asked what he knew about Jesus. He replied, "I haven't got to that yet." A Sunday-school which has not "got to that yet," amid its many schemes and plans and picnics, is false to its trust.

To PRESENT CHRIST, then, is our object in Sunday-school work. How shall we vividly and savingly present him to the heart? By universal consent the senses must usher truth to the soul.

The Sunday-school works mainly through the two most influential senses, sight and hearing. Hearing lacks vividness without sight; sight lacks definiteness without hearing. It is well, therefore, that hearing and seeing should accompany each other. Joseph's brethren brought to their father, who had long mourned for Joseph as dead, this wonderful message: "Thus saith thy son Joseph, I am yet alive; come down unto me, tarry not." Jacob's heart fainted when he simply *heard* these words, for he believed them not; but "when he *saw the wagons* which Joseph had sent to carry him, the spirit of Jacob their father revived." The wagons would have meant nothing unless they had been preceded by the message; the message would have failed unless it had been followed by the wagons. This shows us how to use the eye and ear in the Sunday-school. Give what "is *written*," and then, by maps, pictures, objects, blackboard exercises, and stories, put it into "wagons" to help the imagination and the understanding. The flowers and butterflies in "Joseph's garden" had no smile of hope, no promise of a resurrection, for Mary, when she came there at that early hour of Easter morning, "while it was *yet dark*" in her heart; but since the message has come, "The Lord is risen indeed," every flower and butterfly has been to the bereaved an object-lesson of the resurrection. Until the announcement of Christ's rising was heard, the grain gave no promise of a future life; but, after that Paul put the whole doctrine of the resurrection into the "seed that falls into the ground and dies" that it may live again.

Thus hearing and seeing should work together. But while "Ear-Gate" has had a well-trodden path by constant use, "Eye-Gate" has rusted on its hinges in neglect. We wish to speak especially of the way to present Christ to the heart through this much-neglected "Eye-Gate."

The *visions* by which God taught his truth were usually more impressive than his *spoken messages.* The words written in fire on the wall at Babylon conveyed God's warning to the King's heart more convincingly than spoken words would have done. Dr. Vincent found it hard to get his little boy to eat bread and butter until, one morning, after spreading a slice of bread, he cut it into bread-logs and piled it up in the shape of a house, and then very quickly "down came the house," and all was eaten!

Put the "bread of heaven" into object-lessons and visible illustrations, and the many hearts who find it hard to realize the truth they hear will eagerly receive it and understand it. Talk about the power of God's promises in general terms, and it may all be forgotten. Make the picture of a key on the blackboard and write on it "Promise," and then tell the story of the "key of promise" and Doubting Castle, and you will make the oldest and youngest hearers feel the preciousness and power of God's promises; or, picture a bunch of keys of different sizes and write a promise on each one, and then you can tell those to whom you speak that God's promises fit every experience of life and unlock every difficulty—and every hearer will grasp and keep the thought.

Eye-Teaching is Philosophical.

All of the senses *seem* to merge themselves in sight. As each of the four fingers is exactly opposite the thumb, so each of the other four senses seems to connect itself with sight. We say of food that we have been describing, "*Taste and see;*" we say of the fragrance of a flower of which we have been speaking, "*Smell and see;*" we say of some excellent singer whose voice we have eulogized, "*Hear and see;*" or of a gem we have called very smooth, "*Feel and see.*" In a new sense, "It is *all in your eye.*" Whether it be music or perfume, we say, "*Come and see;*" whether it be bread or stone, we say, "Try and *see.*" Even of questions in our minds we say, "Let me *see;*" and if the matter be obscure, "I can't *see* it." This is because *we think by images*, by something we can *see*, or *imagine that we see.* It is a craving of the mind that makes "the *likes*" necessary in every kind of teaching. The unknown must be taught by *likening* it to something that is known; the unseen must be represented by the seen.

Modern primers teach the unknown word by placing it beside the picture of the object it represents. The picture of a dog will aid the little scholar to remember the word "Dog." We used to say, "D stands for Dog;" rather was it "Dog (the picture) stands for D." Half of our childhood knowledge comes in rhymes about the "*likes.*" Rev. Dr. M'Cook gives a happy example of this in his work on "Object and Outline Teaching:"

> "As red as a cherry, as brisk as a bee,
> As brown as a berry, as tall as a tree,
> As sweet as a pink, as bitter as gall,
> As black as ink, as round as a ball," etc.

Try to teach a child what "red" is without this implied or real object-teaching, with nothing but words to describe what it is, and the child will have as poor an idea of it as the blind man, who, after a long explanation of this color, concluded it must be "*very much like the sound of a trumpet.*" Hold up the cherry to the child, and the lesson is learned in a moment. This same method follows us into a completer education. Maps, specimens, blackboards, slates, etc., are found even in the highest grades of teaching. Though a man have spoken his words never so eloquently, the hearers want him, if possible, to have "*something to show for it.*" A figure is more easily retained than an abstract truth. So deeply grounded is this fact in our nature that we think by figures and pictures. Indeed, language itself is *fossil pictures*, rather than "fossil poetry," as Emerson calls it. Letters were originally hieroglyphics, and hieroglyphics are only pictures used as symbols. When we add something *shown* to something *spoken*, we only add a picture for the eye to a picture for the imagination.

Eye-Teaching Scriptural.

Dr. Vincent, in the preface to his recent work on "The Church School," says: "The good philanthropists of the last century, in digging that they might build a human fabric, laid bare an ancient and divine foundation." These words, spoken of the modern Sunday-school, are especially true of its eye-teaching. It is not "a new idea," but an "ancient and divine foundation" laid bare for us to build upon to-day.

The Bible is full of object-lessons taught by God himself, by Christ, and by the inspired writers, with trees, stars, shields, girdles, fruits, birds, pictures, etc., as their texts and illustrations. The broken tree teaches the fate of the wicked, the withered tree that of the idle, the fruitful tree that of the righteous. The "empty vine" teaches us of the unfaithful, the vine of "wild grapes" of the wicked, the vine of "good fruit" of those who abide in Christ. The star represents the Messiah, also those who turn many to righteousness. The rent garment, the rotten girdle, the "naughty figs," etc., are used to represent wickedness and God's dealings with it. In fact, the Bible is an "illuminated missal," as Chapin calls it, in every page full of pictures and object-teaching.

God himself is our precedent in this kind of instruction. Take, for instance, his teachings of Jeremiah, "*What seest thou*, Jeremiah?" (Jer. i, 11; xxiv, 3;) or his great object-lesson given to Peter on the housetop at Joppa, (Acts x, 9, etc.) Any one interested in following out this study may find other cases where God himself taught his truth by this method of eye-teaching in the following passages, many of which the teacher can adapt to his own use:

Jer. xiii, 1–11, The marred girdle; xviii, 1–6, The potter's vessel; xix, 1–11, The broken bottle; xxvii, 1–11, Bonds and yokes; xliii, 8–10, Stones in the clay; li, 63, 64, The stone and the book; Ezek. iv, 1–8; Blackboard exercise on a tile; v, The hair and the punishment of wrong; xxxvii, 1–14, Dry bones; xxxvii, 15–28, Sticks; xlvii, 1–12, Waters; Dan. ii, 31–45, The great image; Gen. ii, 16, 17, Teaching the knowledge of good and evil by means of commands associated with a tree; Jonah iv, 4–11, God's pity for the wicked taught with a gourd; Gen. xxii, 1–14, A dramatic object-lesson to teach trust in God; xv, 5, 6, Stars; lx, 9–26, Heifer, etc. Moses recognized the blackboard idea when he said of Scripture texts to the Israelites, "Thou shalt write them upon the posts of thy house and on thy gates."

The illustrations of eye-teaching in the life of our "Great Teacher" are no less abundant. Wayside wells, mountain lilies, flying clouds, vineyards, harvest-fields, every thing that met his eye, was turned into Gospel, as Midas turned every thing he touched into gold. He even caused a tree to wither away to use it as an object-lesson for his disciples! Beecher says of this act and others of his object-lessons:

"As to his condemning the tree, it was not a judicial sentence. We are not to suppose that our Saviour summoned the tree into judgment, and argued upon it as if it were a moral being under condemnation or under penalty. No; the whole plot and plan of the ancient mode of teaching forbids that interpretation of it. It is but an acted parable. And this is an important thought, because in many instances in Christ's life, the same mode of teaching was resorted to.

"For example, when he cleansed the temple, undoubtedly the whole act was a parabolic act. He drove out the cattle; he overturned the money-changers' tables; he commanded those that had doves to take them thence. And the whole was not a mere formal attempt at the reformation of the ad ministration of the temple, but a series of acts which indicated the purification of religion—the change that was going on. And, as usual, it was a kind of parabolic action. As a parable is a picture in words, conveying not a moral lesson—not a truth narrated—but simply an artificial picture, drawn for the sake of certain moral results which were to flow from it, so certain of Christ's actions were dramatic. They were, as it were, a momentary drama, enacted for the sake of the truth that they would convey. The most impressive one of all these is the Transfiguration, in which, with Peter, James, and John, he went to the mountain, where, while he was praying, they fell asleep. When they awoke they saw two angelic, or celestial personages, standing and talking with him. And his countenance was changed. Then they communed with him concerning his coming death. The whole was to those disciples a picture of the event. It was not so much a prophetic representation to interpret it to them as a pictorial representation to fortify their minds, so that when their earthly hopes, which were centered in him, should be dashed, they would be bold, and maintain faith in him. It was a kind of enacted celestial parable, or picture, or tableau.

"So here, when going in the morning to Jerusalem, Jesus saw the fig-tree and observed that it was in full leaf. Evidently it was a prematurely early one. And why should he go to see if there were figs upon it? Because sometimes a tree bore winter figs, which became ripe in early spring; and perhaps he might have expected that there would be some on that one which he might glean. But when he came to it, and found that there were no figs, but leaves only, he said, 'Let no fruit grow on thee henceforward forever, and let no man eat fruit of thee.'

"That this was said in a very impressive manner is evident by the fact that when, the day after, the disciples returned that way, they remembered the occurrence, and called his attention to the tree. Doubtless he designed that this should be a very solemn instruction to them.

"But what was the instruction? They were every day going backward and forward to and from Jerusalem. There he went into the sacred precinct, or into the part of it which was Herod's great porch—the Basilica, as it was called. There he used to teach the people. All around about him were the insignia of Jewish worship, and his very business was to expose the superficialities of life in these things. He was, from day to day, attempting to carry them back to the reality of a religious life, to a deeper moral tone, to a more earnest conscientiousness. It was his business to reprehend the self-conceit and moral complacency which passed itself off upon mere superficial observers. And here was an opportunity. Here happened to be, of all the trees that stood in the road on that early spring day, one that had come into full leaf. But when he went up to it he found no fruit on it, but leaves only—nothing but leaves. It was just exactly like those over the other side. All of them were full of leaves, but not one of them—neither priest, nor scribe, nor Pharisee, nor Sadducee—bore any fruit. All of them were clothed with leaves, but none of them were fruitful. Here was a symbol, here was an opportunity of illustrating a fact by a parabolic action. By destroying that tree with a word he could impress upon his disciples that which would be a benefit to them in their teachings of men for ever after. And he did it."

Study the sermon on the mount with a view of observing its eye-teaching. The Emancipation Proclamation has been so written that the shading of the letters forms a picture of President Lincoln, which seems to lie beneath the writing. So in this sermon on the mount, by the vividness of its local illustrations, we see a picture of Christ sitting on the mountain, and pointing with his finger to the objects in sight, as he draws from each its appropriate lesson; and not only do we see the finger of Christ, but in and under the sermon we find a map of the scenery all about him, with its cities, its trees, its birds, its flowers, and even its weeds, sketched upon it.

Notice the sermon in this light. Wishing to impress upon the disciples their great responsibility and wide influence, he points them to the city of Safed on the mountains near by, distinctly seen, as the sunlight gilded its walls, and then he says to the disciples, "Ye are the light of the world, *a city* *that is set on a hill that cannot be hid.*" Matt. v, 14. Then he turns and calls the attention of the multitude to the narrow and wide gates of the city.* Through the narrow gate, which is called "the needle's eye," are passing a few foot-passengers, and a camel now and then enters, but only by bowing down and leaving his burden outside the gate: on the other hand, through the large city gates flows the gulf stream of business and the eager multitude of tradesmen. Christ applies the scene to his sermon: "Enter ye in at the strait gate: for wide is the gate, and broad is the way, that leadeth to destruction, and many there be which go in thereat: because strait is the gate, and narrow is the way, which leadeth unto life, and few there be that find it." Matt. vii, 13, etc. Beware, O ye rich men! for you can only enter the kingdom of heaven as the camel passes the needle's eye, by bowing at the gate, and leaving your burden behind.

Then he seems to turn his eyes more to the natural objects about him, and translates their lessons to the disciples. The sparrows that sing among the olive-trees of the mountain attract his attention, and he points to them that he may teach the watchcare of Providence: "Are not five sparrows sold for two farthings, and not one of them is forgotten before God? Fear not therefore: ye are of more value than many sparrows." Luke xii, 6, 7. Then another flock of birds attracts his attention, and he uses them to still further enforce this thought of God's care: "Consider the ravens: for they neither sow nor reap; which neither have storehouse nor barn; and God feedeth them: how much more are ye better than the fowls?" Luke xii, 24. Then he weaves the vines and trees, and also the thistles and thorns, of the mountain into a lesson of diligence in showing faith by works: "Ye shall know them by their fruits. Do men gather grapes of thorns or figs of thistles?" The cloud that appears in sight also bears him a message: "And he said, When ye see a cloud

* We use the familiar explanation of the "needle's eye," although there is division of opinion between this explanation and others.

2

rise out of the west, straightway ye say, There cometh a shower; and so it is. Ye hypocrites, ye can discern the face of the sky and of the earth; but how is it that ye do not discern this time?"—the spiritual truth of my mission. Best of all, he impressed the lesson of God's personal watchcare, which he had taught by the sparrows and ravens, by turning to the beautiful white lilies of Palestine that bloomed abundantly about him, and saying: *Consider* the lilies; observe them carefully; take their lesson to heart; read it over and over. Consider the lilies: how abundantly they grow, how prosperously they grow, how mysteriously they grow. Consider the beauty of the lilies: Solomon in all the glory of his royal white robe was not arrayed with such beauty as this snowy lily. Wherefore, if God so *adorn* the grass and flowers of the field, which quickly fade, and are cast with the dry straw and withered herbs and stubble into the oven for fuel, how much more will he clothe you, O ye of little faith! The sparrows are almost worthless, and yet God watches over their *lives;* the ravens have no storehouse, yet our Father provides their *food;* the lilies toil not, and yet the Father gives them *raiment.* And shall not He who takes such care of the fowls in his yard and the plants in his garden much more clothe and care for you, who are the children of his fireside?

As the sibyl wrote her prophecies on leaves, so Jesus has written his truth on the lily blossom, the raven's wing, the ruby grape, the white grain, the passing cloud, the narrow and wide gates, the city of the hill-top, the water of the wayside well, and the fruit of the orchard. The Indians have a legend, mentioned in Hiawatha, that—

> "All the wild flowers of the forest,
> All the lilies of the prairie,
> When on earth they fade and perish,
> Blossom in the rainbow o'er us:
> 'Tis the heaven of flowers you see there."

Christ, on the other hand, took the heavenly rainbow of truth and put it into the "wild flowers" and "lilies" of earth.

Sandalphon, the angel of prayer, says the legend,

"Gathers our prayers as he stands,
And they turn into flowers in his hands."

The great Teacher shows us how we may take the flowers in our hands and *turn them into prayers.*

Were it necessary, it might be interesting to show in this connection how the Tabernacle was a great school for object-lessons, each part of it teaching the people a word of high import. As the child in his primer sees the *picture* of a house, and learns the *word* "House" below it the more readily, so God showed the people a bloody altar, and wrote under it that great word, "Atonement;" he showed them a laver of pure water, and taught them the word "Purity;" he showed them a golden candlestick, and taught them "Light;" the lamb was a prophecy of "the Lamb of God;" the vail, of Christ's flesh. God was teaching the unseen and eternal by the seen and temporal. These altars and lavers, etc., were but "*figures* of the true." The whole book of Hebrews teaches through these object-lessons. Christ himself was not only a sacrifice for us, but was also a grand visible lesson, illustrating to man how the characteristics of God could be "made *manifest* in the flesh." God gave to men this privilege of seeing Christ in answer to that feeling that made it the intensest longing of the prophets and sweetest memory of the apostles to "*see* Jesus." The world desired to "*behold* the Lamb," unsatisfied, like Simeon, until it had "*seen* God's salvation." The Bible is the greatest text-book and store-house of object-lessons in the world. Every sacrifice and feast of the Old Testament, and every sacrament of the New, is an object-lesson. The Sabbath is an object-lesson of creation, and also of heaven; the rainbow after the flood, the moving pillar in the wilderness, and every vision of prophecy, are object-lessons, and the 119th Psalm is an acrostic of Hebrew letters.

Eye-Teaching Adapted to the Times.

We need only to refer to the increased amount of blackboard work in our day-schools, to the large number of magazines and papers that have recently introduced illustrations into their heretofore unillustrated pages, to the inscriptions on rocks and fences, the great number of picture advertisements in our papers, and the increasing custom of illustrating lectures, to remind our readers that one marked characteristic of this age is an inclination to put things into the mind by a quick concentration on the eye. We must "discern the signs of the times" and keep up with them. We must study times and men. The advertising pages, which are epitomized photographs of the day, and the "Bitters" on stones, "Buchu" on trees, and "Magic Oil" on every thing, notwithstanding their quackery, teach us that this age must be reached very much through the eye.

With Whom should Eye-Teaching be Used?

Not with the little children alone by any means, nor with the ignorant simply. Christ used it in teaching the rich and wise Nicodemus. He taught him the greatest truth that man can ever learn by reminding him of the serpent lifted up in the wilderness, and using that as an object-lesson to teach him of redemption and regeneration. Paul was not too old or learned, after he had graduated from "the feet of Gamaliel," to be taught by an object-lesson. "As we tarried [at Cesarea] there many days, there came down from Judea a certain prophet, named Agabus. And when he was come unto us, he took Paul's girdle, and bound his own hands and feet, and said, Thus saith the Holy Ghost, So shall the Jews at Jerusalem bind the man that owneth this girdle." Acts xxi, 10, 11. God came to teach even the eloquent Peter, not exactly with outlines on a blackboard, but with "all manner of beasts in a sheet let down from heaven." The blackboard and object-lesson are as necessary in a school where there are many adults as in an infant-school. All feel the power of this God-given method of presenting the truth to the heart.

WHENCE SHALL ILLUSTRATIONS BE GATHERED?

In answer to this question we give an extract from an admirable address by Rev. Stephen H. Tyng, Jun., on the subject of illustration:—

"1. Let them be gathered from the word of God itself. The writers of the seventeenth century used Scripture to illustrate Scripture. Every thing in this book, the Bible, is there by divine choice. There is nothing not intended to be used to illustrate some positive truth. There is nothing so direct in addressing the minds of children as the similes of Scripture. Speaking of the judgment-day, can you find any thing that more admirably illustrates it than the thief in the night? Speaking of servants, is there any thing illustrating it more perfectly than the yoke, of which God bears a part? Take the parables, those matchless portions of Christ's own wisdom, which go to interpret the force of every thing in this world. . . . The Old Testament illustrations and quotations were used by Christ in his life, on the cross, and we also find them in the Revelation after Christ's ascension. In using illustrations take them from the Bible, and tell them in your own language. Bunyan's 'Pilgrim's Progress' is based on the Old and New Testaments. Illustrations from nature may also be employed. You may have the beautiful parable of Gotthold. A piece of clay was placed by the side of a tea-rose, and when removed it had absorbed the fragrance of the rose. What teaches better than this the relation we bear to Jesus? Take the parable of Jean Paul Richter. Walking in his garden in the morning, he saw the pearly dew-drop on the leaf. In the evening he went out to look at the dew-drop, and found that it had gone. He looked about and saw the rainbow in the heavens. This he used to illustrate the death of little children, and to show how they are transplanted from this beauteous earth to reappear with greater beauty in the heavens. Form your parable from things you see. 2. Keep within the range of the scholar's observation. If there is any thing I abhor in a Sunday-school it is a fixture. I have had people tell the same stories which I have heard ever since childhood, and they told them as occurring in their own experience. There's a great danger in telling old stories. 3. Keep within the region of probabilities. Some people tell such improbable stories that the children can't believe them. Be jealous for the truth. 4. Some men have a habit of saying things out of place. I knew a man who had a story about noise, and told it on every possible occasion. When in company he would stamp his foot and say, 'There's a noise. O, speaking of noise reminds me of a story,' and then he would proceed with it. Some men thus use every opportunity to make a nail to hang a story on, even if it does not fit into the lesson. 5. People hang on to stories too long. When you are done with stories, drop them. Of what use is the scaffold after the building is completed?"

Rev. Wm. M. Taylor, D.D., says on the same subject: "There is no faculty more susceptible of development by culture than that of discovering analogies. The study of the sermons of those men who are most remarkable for the pertinence of their illustrations will be of service to you—not by furnishing you with analogies ready-made, but by showing you what treasures are lying all around you. We may paraphrase here the inscription on Wren's monument, and say, '*Si illustrationes quœris circumspice.*' You will find them every-where—in the talk of the children and the shouts of the school-boys; on the street and in the store; on the ship and in the railroad car; in the field of Nature and on the page of literature. Only compel yourself for a time to look at every thing with the question uppermost, 'What use can I make of that in commending the truth of Christ to my fellow-men?' and by and by you will have so formed the habit that, unconsciously and without any effort on your part, the finest analogies will strike you."

WHO SHALL CONDUCT EYE-TEACHING?

That which is to be given before the whole school should be conducted by the pastor, if he is the best man for such work, or by the superintendent, or by a selected teacher. Let the best workman be selected whatever his position. One may be best in object-teaching, another in blackboard work. In the latter not only skill in using chalk is to be considered, but also and especially ability to talk the subject sweetly into the hearts of those that hear. One may design the exercises and talk about them, having another who is a better artist to do the mechanical work. If there is an artist in the school, enlist his talent for Christ. "God sends us an artist, and he immediately becomes a blackboardist," said an enthusiastic Sunday-school pastor to a new member. And the artist recognized the Master's call to labor, and his heart answered, "Here am I, Lord;" and from that hour the Sunday-school was the fortunate possessor of consecrated ability, displayed in the matter of exquisitely beautiful blackboard illustrations done in colored crayons. "He spends the whole of every Sunday afternoon in the exhaustive study of the lesson. When he has it *all by heart*, he makes a pencil sketch of the design of the picture that he means to furnish us with on the following Sunday. The first fresh hours of each morning of the week he gives to the work of drawing and coloring the large blackboard illustration so prized by our school; and he adds the last loving, finishing touches to the whole on Sunday, just before bringing it up to the school."

Usually a simple outline sketch or word exercise would be better than such a picture, but if God gives you an artist, use him. Why not have a picture for the school on the blackboard as well as on the wall? We cannot, however, emphasize too strongly the fact that object-lessons and blackboard exercises should, as a rule, be very simple, lest the *means* by which we teach shall draw the attention from the *truth* to be taught. When Moses and Elias, on the Mount of Transfiguration, divided and diverted the attention of the apostles from Christ, they were removed from sight, and the apostles "saw no man save Jesus only." Let the object-lessons vanish if they divert the eye from Jesus; let the blackboard fall, like Peter, James, and John, to the ground, if it stands between the scholars' hearts and Christ. Amid all these helps let the Sunday-school "hear Him" above all other voices.

What shall Give us Themes for Eye-Teaching?

Three things should usually have weight in selecting a map, story, or object-lesson, or in making a blackboard exercise: 1. The lesson of the school or class; 2. The events of the day; 3. The time of the year. While the lesson should usually be the center of the eye-teaching, yet, at times, striking and special events of the day or the season of the year may suggest other themes that will be impressive. If there is a temperance excitement, exercises on temperance might for a day be better than an exercise on the subject of the lesson. So in time of flowers, fruits, or autumn leaves, the season rather than the lesson may give the eye-teacher his theme.

Divisions of Eye-Teaching.

Taking the subject in a comprehensive view, we make the following divisions:

I. Vivid Description and Allegories.
II. Stories Vividly Told.
III. Stories Represented.
IV. Religious Object-Teaching.
V. Map-Teaching.
VI. Picture-Teaching.
VII. Blackboard Exercises.
1. Motto Exercise.
2. Topic Exercise.
3. Initial Exercise.
4. Syllable Exercise.
5. Word Exercise.
6. Phrase Exercise.
7. Table Exercise.
8. Acrostic Exercise.
9. Parallel and Contrast Exercise.
10. Canceling Exercise.
11. Erasing Exercise.
12. Word-Symbol Exercise.
13. Map Exercise.
14. Outline Exercise

I. Vivid Description and Allegories.

"The imagination is second to no other faculty in the human mind in understanding God's word. An illustration is only an appeal to the imagination. Imagination is that faculty which sees the hidden truths. It stands before the violet and sees humility. It looks up at the sun and sees truth. When we have to teach the children so much that cannot be seen, the best way is to bring them up to the truth by things which appeal to the imagination."*

"The Bible is not a system of theology; still less is it a creed; but it is a succession of vivid pictures—a true history of living, thinking human beings and of God's dealings with them. Some have said that Sunday-school teachers should not teach geography, history, manners and customs, but only the Gospel. Without these things there is no Gospel. It is impossible to understand God's dealings with any man in the Bible without knowing all about that man's manner of life and surroundings. We must be able to see Abraham sitting at the door of his tent, with his white hair and beard. We must know him as neither more nor less than an Arab sheik, with the intellect of a child, and less knowledge than one of our Sunday-school children. We shall then, and then only, be able to understand God's dealings with him, and what he accomplished by him." †

A scene may be described with the vividness of an eyewitness if it has been carefully studied with the aid of books and pictures. Judge Jay, of Ohio, in company at Washington, conversing with a lady who had traveled in Scotland, was remarking on objects of interest in that country. The judge described Arthur's Seat, the Carleton Hills, and other places so minutely and graphically, that the lady said to him, "When did you visit Scotland?" He said, "*Never.*" "How then can you describe its places so vividly?" He replied, "I have studied them carefully in pictures and descriptions."

* Rev. S. H. Tyng, Jun., D.D. † Rev. Dr. Duryea.

The scenes of the Bible, if vividly described from a thorough knowledge and sympathy with the circumstances, form a picture, a drama, that may properly be classed as eye-teaching. If the teacher is talking about Paul on Mars' Hill, let the surrounding scenes be so described that the scholar can put himself in Paul's place and make the scene real. Let the doctrines of the Epicureans and Stoics be so distinctly described that the application of every sentence shall be felt. If the Good Samaritan be the subject, let the teachers make the scholars feel the very shadow of the rocks on that dangerous way, and the moisture of the cloth with which the blood is wiped from the arms of the man left half dead. The Epistle to the Corinthians may be made as beautiful to the eye as a temple by a thorough understanding of the architecture of Ephesus, *from* which Paul wrote, and of Corinth, *to* which he wrote.

In fact, whatever the lesson may be, if all the geographical and historical knowledge connected with it is clustered around it there will be a picturesqueness and vividness that will add greatly to its power. Take the following illustration of this kind of description on the subject of FEEDING THE MULTITUDE:

The incident has its lesson for the pews as well as its encouragement for the pulpit. Christ might have scattered this heavenly manna, as of old, by the same miraculous power that multiplied it. He chose rather to use human agency, and "gave it to the disciples, and they gave it to the multitude." There was a great variety of tastes, talents, and dispositions among the disciples; but Christ used them all, not merely to distribute the bread, but also to impress its lesson. There was the loving John, the impulsive Peter, the doubting Thomas, the systematic Matthew, the law-loving James, and the others, each with some trait of character peculiarly his own. Sometimes, as I have thought of this incident, I have imagined the different feelings with which the disciples received the bread and thought of the miracle. John, as he took the loaves, would stand and look with his deep, loving eyes upon Jesus, almost forgetting the multitude as he gazed, "lost in wonder, love, and praise," upon his Master. Impulsive Peter would seize the loaves eagerly and hurry about, scattering them hastily among the multitude, and, with his emphasis and love of prophecy, proclaiming on every hand that they saw the promise fulfilled, "He shall feed his flock like a shepherd." James, with his love of the old law, would remind the people, as he scattered the bread, that the same power that fed their fathers in the wilderness was feeding them on the shores of Galilee. Systematic Matthew would remind the people how greatly the loaves had been multiplied and how many had been fed; while Thomas, as he took the bread from Jesus, would press his thumbs into the loaves that he might be assured he was not dreaming, and that he did not hold a phantom in his hand, meanwhile glancing cautiously at the Master, and whispering to his nearest friend, "What manner of man is this?"

Christ used all these various talents to get the bread and its lesson to the multitude; and so to-day the bread which is given to you with Christ's blessing from the written Word, the Spirit, and the Gospel ministry, God expects you to scatter among the multitude in your daily walks, around your firesides, along your waysides, and in your places of business.

"Give ye them to eat."

The sermons of Rev. T. De Witt Talmage abound in examples of vivid description of Bible scenes, and may profitably be studied by teachers as models in this respect.

The plan of representing abstract truths in concrete forms, and personifying the ideal, so beautifully illustrated by the parables of our Lord, and also by the fables of Æsop and the allegories of Bunyan and others, may often be used to great advantage by the Sunday-school teacher. Dr. Eggleston once told a company of children of a house that a king had built with two beautiful windows, two wonderful servants, etc., to which that king sent his son, and the man who lived in the king's house refused to let him in; in short, making the human body and soul an allegorical house, and describing it in such a way that the children could surmise, before he finished the description, that he was talking of them and Christ's coming for admittance to their hearts.

Gifts from a Casket.—[This exercise, contributed by Rev. W. E. Huntington, shows very well how abstract truth may be presented in an attractive verbal form.] A speaker addressing a body of children desires to talk of some of the virtues and graces that should adorn character. Let him tell the children he has some gifts to distribute to them. He has a ring for each finger on both hands. Then, holding up the first finger of his left hand, let him call the ring for that finger Obedience, for example, and ask the children to repeat the word in unison. A story may be told illustrative of this virtue. And so on for each finger of both hands. This list may be used for the rings: Obedience, Truthfulness, Courtesy, Kindness, Cheerfulness, Humility, Temperance, Love. Calling these virtues rings, and slipping them upon their fingers, in imagination, will prove to be the best way of fastening the lessons to be taught upon the memories of children. Their attention may be held more closely by frequently asking them to repeat the names of the rings in concert, following the order in which they have been given. Then, as they will want to show these gifts to their friends, they must have sandals upon their feet. Call these sandals Courage. Let them repeat this word in a full, clear voice. Show how without these sandals it would be useless to try to wear some of the rings—Obedience and Temperance, for instance. Then give them a girdle of Christlikeness, showing how, as a girdle binds the garments closely about one, that he may run or work well, so Christlikeness is a comprehensive quality of character that will enable us to live well. Lastly, place the crown of Faith upon their heads. Speak of faith as the highest ornament of character. It links us to God, and therefore ought to be placed above all others, as a crowning grace. Then let the names of the rings, of the sandals, of the girdle, of the crown, be repeated in concert, and the speaker may close by telling his audience of little hearers that these ornaments are of finer stuff than silver or gold, and will not wear out nor tarnish by wearing them every day, but will only grow brighter by use, and that they come from God's casket of jewels—the Bible.*

II.—STORIES VIVIDLY TOLD.

The great teachers of the race are those who have clothed truth in stories of some kind. Æsop, Bunyan, Beecher, Spurgeon, and a host of others, are examples of this class. A man gave to Christ, as he thought, a troublesome question, "Who is my neighbor?" It was answered vividly with the story of the good Samaritan.

Jews regarded with scorn the "publicans and sinners" that had accepted Christ. Jesus taught them their duty by the prodigal's story. Ralph Wells writes: "I asked a young woman upon the street, 'What portion of the Scripture did you the most good?' She replied, 'That which does all men good, the parable of the prodigal son. It is so pleasant, so plain! There stands the father with outstretched arms. It is wonderful, the love of Jesus Christ for the sinner!'" Stories vividly told, put on as a garment, are a part of eye-teaching. The teacher should be amply supplied with them. "Where will you go to-day?" said a mother to her little

* The author has heard the writer of the above form a group of allegorical statuary of the virtues: Valor, as a true soldier, first set up, and then Knowledge, as a true scholar; Temperance, as a man of strength and health and manliness; and so, following with Patience, Brotherly-Kindness, Faith, and Love, making them seem like a group of statues upon the platform around him as he described their characteristics, and giving some incident illustrative of each one after describing it

girl, "to Aunt Mary's or Aunt Jane's?" She replied, "I will go to see Aunt Jane, for she always has plenty of ginger snaps and keeps them on the lowest shelf." The teacher should have plenty of stories and "keep them on the lowest shelf," so that children can understand them; a note-book and pencil always with him and a scrap-book at home will easily gather the "snaps."

This is good advice from a teacher: "Use the pencil. It is easy to carry. It aids the memory. It catches and keeps a thousand flitting thoughts. Carry a small blank book. If you see a fact or think a thought that may be of any possible use in the future take note of it. You may not *now* see of what service it can be, but when interested in a lesson you may glance over the penciled jottings and find one, two, ten helpful illustrations or allusions, the worth of which, in the exposition of your subject, may be invaluable. One fact a day thus taken into captivity will register three hundred and sixty-five a year—so many servitors in your work. Use the pencil."

Henry Clay Trumbull writes these excellent words about telling Bible stories vividly: "It has been urged by some earnest Sunday-school writer that children should never be trapped into hearing a Bible story, by its recital in homely language, as if it were from another source than the Book of God. But there are two sides to even that question. If a child is disinclined to hear Bible stories, it is not fair to assume you are telling him something else when he is sure to find at the close that you have palmed off one of the obnoxious narratives in another garb. On the other hand, it is eminently desirable to so clothe the Bible history to children as to give to the persons and incidents thereof a naturalness and reality that is not secured to little folks through the somewhat obsolete forms of our common English version. What would be wrong for purposes of deception is quite proper for the purpose of elucidation.

"An incident in my own experience confirms my opinion on this point. I well recall the time when I had far more reverence for than understanding of the Bible. Scripture characters were to me not only mythical but unintelligible. The difference between Genesis and Euroclydon was by no means clear to my mind. I did not know who Deuteronomy was, nor what was Jehoshaphat. The first dawn of clear day came in this way. My home was by the sea-side, where figures of sailor life were familiar to all. One afternoon a good man came to our Sabbath-school gathering, and, entering the desk by request of the superintendent, commenced to tell a story. He described a sea-shore scene, with a vessel in the offing weighing anchor and loosing sail for a voyage. Vividly, in word painting, he showed a boat putting off from the dock, bringing at the last moment a passenger for the trip, his clambering on to the dock, the start of the vessel, its progress, a gathering storm, danger on the deep, the fright of passengers and crew, a consultation, and the confession of the late-coming passenger that he was a fugitive pursued of God for his sin, hence the storm and the peril to all. O how well I remember the new light that burst into my mind when I then recognized the hitherto unreal story of Jonah as a living verity! I felt as did the boy who at last saw Lafayette through the carriage window, and called out in amazement, 'Why, he's only a *man!*' 'Jonah' had been *Jonah* to me until that hour. Now he was a *man.* 'Joppa' had been *Joppa.* Now it was a *sea-port town.* My little brain was almost bewildered with the discovery that the Bible had something in it that I could understand; but the vail of mystery that had enwrapped it until then went overboard with Jonah when that Sunday-school speaker had him thrown into the sea in the story. The entrance of God's words gave me light just as soon as those words were so stated that they could enter my child-mind. I am confident that I should not have been so profited at that time had the narrator announced in commencing that he was to tell us a Bible story. His course may, I think, be safely commended to many a teacher of the young.

"At the Newsboys' Lodging House in New York, ten years ago, I heard Mr. Tracy, the then Superintendent, entrap, as some might call it, his motley audience into hearing a Bible story when they would not have listened quietly to his reverent reading of the sacred narrative. Commencing the parable of the prodigal son, he told it in what would have seemed slang phrase to others, but in language which was really the vernacular of those boys. He held their fixed attention as he proceeded, and when their interest was most intense he said suddenly:

"But, boys, this story is all written out in a book I have here. Let me read you the rest of it.' And he opened the Bible and continued the narration, reading and explaining or translating by turn. Who shall say he was irreverent, or caused his hearers to be?"

III.—STORIES REPRESENTED.

Stories that are read may sometimes be a little vivified by using or showing something mentioned in the story. In telling the story of Joseph when he sent the message to Jacob, a piece of brown paper (which will represent parchment) may be cut into a foot square and rolled up as a Jewish scroll, with this letter written upon it, to be read after the scroll is described and the circumstances narrated—Gen. xlv, 9, etc.:

EGYPT, 1706.

JACOB ISRAEL,—Thus saith thy son Joseph: I am yet alive. Come down to me; tarry not; and thou shalt be near to me, and I will nourish thee.

JOSEPH, *Lord of all Egypt.*

This letter should be written with the lines slanting very much, as the slant in Jewish letters indicates love.

With this story of Joseph the passage from Revelation may be read: "Fear not: I am he that liveth and was dead, and behold, I am alive for evermore." This may be used to show that Joseph was not dead, although unseen; so Christ is not dead, but "ever lives above." Other analogies may also be brought out—for example, the Lord is our Shepherd, and has also become a King, and we "shall not want."

The stories of the Bible can often be told with some Eastern or missionary relic to illustrate them, or something resembling objects mentioned in the accounts: the parable of the vineyard with a bunch of grapes, Joseph's dream with a handful of wheat, Stephen's death with a pile of stones, Joseph sold for twenty pieces of silver with a handful of coin, the tribute money scene with a piece of money, etc. A preacher, in speaking about the heathen, took a heathen god from his pocket and intensified his words by bringing the simple object into his story at the right time.*

IV.—RELIGIOUS OBJECT-TEACHING.

We shall try to answer five questions that are often asked in regard to object-teaching in the Sunday-school: 1. *What* is religious object-teaching? 2. *Why* should it be used? 3. *When* should it be used? 4. *Where* shall we obtain objects? and, 5. *How* shall we use them?

What is religious object-teaching? We can most readily show what it is by comparing it with the well-known object-teaching of our best day-schools.

In the day-school an object is presented to the eye—a leaf, a flower, a mineral, a fossil, or a bone—to be studied for its own sake, and the lesson is perfect only when every quality

* Rev. J. S. Ostrander has prepared a box of "Oriental Block Models" that enable the teacher to give at once a cheap, accurate, and vivid representation, in their real forms, of the tabernacle, temple, Jewish house, wine-press, and other specimens of Bible architecture. Any part of the Bible that has architectural references may be most effectively illustrated by this ingenious arrangement.

and attribute of the object is known. In the Sunday-school, on the other hand, the object, although it may be any of those mentioned above, is studied as a symbol, a suggestion, a picture of some thought or idea far above itself, and the lesson is perfect when the attention is secured by the object, and the one or two qualities that may illustrate the thought which is being presented are understood.

We may illustrate the day-school object-teaching by a recitation at DOTHEBOY'S HALL:

"'This is the first class in English spelling and philosophy, Nickleby,' said Squeers, beckoning Nicholas to stand beside him. 'Now, then, where's the first boy?'

"'Please, sir, he's cleaning the back parlor window,' said the temporary head of the philosophical class.

"'So he is, to be sure,' rejoined Squeers. 'We go upon the practical mode of teaching, Nickleby; the regular education system: c-l-e-a-n, clean, verb active, to make bright, to scour. W-i-n, win, d-e-r, der, winder, a casement. When the boy knows this out of a book he goes and does it. It's just the same principle as the use of the globes. Where's the second boy?'

"'Please, sir, he's weeding the garden,' replied a small voice.

"'To be sure,' said Squeers, by no means disconcerted. 'So he is. B-o-t, bot, t-i-n, tin, bottin, n-e-y, ney, bottinney, noun substantive, a knowledge of plants. When he has learned that bottinney means a knowledge of plants he goes and knows 'em. That's our system, Nickleby.'"

Although we should hardly give this as a model lesson, yet it illustrates the great characteristics of object-teaching in day-schools. The lesson is perfect when all the qualities of the weeds and the "winder" are ascertained. When the scholar "goes and knows 'em" they lead to nothing further. Religious object-teaching would lead us to look through the "winder" to something greater beyond; it would point us below the roots and above the blossoms of the plants to the Hand that made them.

The following will exactly illustrate the point we have just mentioned. A boy brought home to his father the teacher's report of his standing, which proved to be much below his usual mark. The father asked him why it was, and he replied that he didn't know. The father knew, however, for he had noticed yellow-covered novels lying about the house during the few days previous. He turned to his son and said, "Empty that basket full of apples upon the floor, and then go out and fill the basket half full of chips."

The son, not suspecting any thing, obeyed. When he had brought the basket half full of chips the father said, "Now put back those apples into the basket." After half of them had been put in they began to roll off. "Put them all in; put them in," said the father sternly.

"I cannot," was the reply.

"Of course you cannot," said the father. "You said you did not know why you had fallen off in standing. Of course, you cannot fill your mind with useful knowledge after getting it half full of that yellow-covered trash you have been reading."

The boy blushed and went away, but never afterward touched one of those novels. In this object-lesson it would have been a waste of time and an injury to the lesson to have had the boy notice any further qualities about chips than the fact that they occupied the room which belonged to more valuable articles. When the object shown in Sunday-school is so used as to make it more prominent than the truth to be taught, it is exalting a "chip" above a moral precept. As much as a flag is less than the loyalty it represents, so much less than the truth presented should the object appear. The highest quality of an object used in Sunday-school teaching is that it should be a perfect mirror, itself almost unnoticed, while reflecting some great idea.

I passed a calm, still lake one starlight night, and beneath its motionless surface there seemed to be "new heavens," the stars were so perfectly reflected in its watery depths, the evening star shining brightest of all. So the religious object-lesson should reflect heavenly things, the Star of Bethlehem always being most prominent in its teachings and suggestions.

2. *Why should object-teaching be used in the Sunday-school?* For the answer to this question the reader is referred to the first pages of this book.

3. *When should object-lessons be used?* (1.) Frequently, as the Saviour used them, lest they shall attract too much attention because of their novelty, and because almost every lesson may be made more interesting at some point by their use. (2.) Only when they may be introduced naturally to help the truth; never as a "side exhibition" attached to the truth rather than an incidental illustration of it.

The younger the scholars, the more frequently should object-lessons be used.

But, 4. *Where shall we get object-lessons?* Generally, not from the books and magazines. The model exercises given in institutes, books, and papers should be read for the suggestions and principles they contain, instead of being literally followed. David in Goliath's hat or Saul's armor would not be more awkward than a teacher often becomes in trying to use, without modification, the object-lesson of another.

The "How," not the "What," should be the question in our minds as we study the object-lessons of others.

For finding object-lessons "the field is the world." The good teacher transforms every phase of life into an illustration. As the delicate plate of the photographer catches a picture of whatever is before it, so the teacher who has put his mind into the illustrative mood catches illustrations from every passing event.

Briefly and rapidly it may be shown how fertile in object-lessons are the fields in which we all walk, how abundant are the lessons within "arm's length" of every day life.. Sitting in my study this very afternoon, let me see how many object-lessons may be found without leaving the room: First, I will search myself. In my breast pocket I find *a letter* from one of our Sunday-school editors promising me a sum of money. The promise would be of no value unless it had a name I could trust signed to it. This letter, then, may be used as an object-lesson to show why we trust in the promises of the Bible: it is because the name of Jesus is signed to them.

In the same pocket is my Berean DAY-BOOK, with a space for every day in the year. The future days are blank, the past days not used as well as they should have been. This object will illustrate the Book of Remembrance, (see Appendix.) In my vest pocket is a *watch.* It may be used as indicated in Appendix. From my pocket I take a *handful of coin.* It may be used to illustrate the story of Joseph sold into slavery, of Christ sold by Judas, or any other incident of Bible history where money is mentioned. On this *two cent piece* is the motto "In God we trust," a good object and text for a talk on God's care of our country. I take out my wallet. Here are some *railroad tickets.* The name of the superintendent signed to them gives me a passport from one place to another. So the name of Jesus gives us a passport to heaven.

This *counterfeit currency* and this *counterfeit bill* also suggest lessons. Sinful pleasure promises to pay us joy "six months after a treaty of peace" between our consciences and sin.

This *life insurance receipt* will illustrate the soul's insurance of heavenly life. Then, this *bunch of keys* is an excellent illustration of God's promises. Starting with the story of "The Key of Promise," I would say that every one of the promises is a key to lock in some treasure, or lock out some enemy, or unlock some store of heavenly wealth. This watch-key suggests the promise with which we "wind up" our trust every day, "As thy days so shall thy strength be." This trunk key represents the traveler's promise, "Lo, I am with you alway;" this house key, "Thou wilt keep him in perfect peace whose mind is stayed on thee;" this church key, "They that wait on the Lord shall renew their strength." This key to my post-office box may represent the promise of prayer, by which we receive God's messages, "Whatsoever ye shall ask in my name I will do it;" this safe key, (if I had one,) "There is that scattereth and yet increaseth;" this skeleton key that will unlock the church door, house door, bed-room door, and many others, the promises that apply to a great variety of cases: "The Lord will provide;" "My grace is sufficient for thee." *My body* may be used as an object-lesson of God's wisdom, for we are all "wonderfully made;" or it may be used allegorically, as in Eccles. xii.

Turning now to my desk and its contents, this white paper is an object-lesson, (see illustration in "Seed-Thought for Object-Lessons.") This sheet of *red blotting paper* may illustrate the promise of the "crimson made white as wool." Formerly men could not whiten crimson rags; from them therefore they must make paper of crimson or some other hue. But Christ can make the crimson stain as white as snow. Here is an *ink bottle* labeled "Ink," but the ink is no longer there. So some persons bear the label "Christian" when the Christlikeness has all disappeared. Here is my *Bible.* It may be used as indicated in "Stories Represented." *My pocket looking-glass,* which I have just taken from a pigeon-hole, is cracked, and therefore makes a poor reflection, as our professedly Christian hearts, when not right in the sight of God, reflect Christ imperfectly. This *photograph* of Abraham Lincoln may be used as indicated in the "Seed-Thought for Object-Lessons."

These *four crackers,* one in the shape of a diamond, another a cross, another a star, another a heart, given me by one of my little friends, were too sacred to eat, and so here they are in this pigeon-hole. In bringing them home the stamp of the name was accidentally broken out of the cross, and the heart, which had no name, was broken on one side. The star and diamond crackers were perfect. Let me try to get a sermon out of these by questioning my little friend,

Alice, who happens to be in my study for a few minutes this afternoon. What are these? "Crackers." What do you see on this star cracker? "Dots." What else? "Letters." What do you think the letters spell? "The name of the man that made it." When do you think the name was stamped on it—when it was soft, or after it was baked? "When it was soft." If they had tried to stamp it when it was hard, what would have happened? "They would break it." [Put the cracker out of sight.] Whose name ought we to have written on our hearts? "Jesus's." When ought it to be written there—when we grow old, or when we are children? "When we are children." When is it easiest to love God? "When we are children." The Bible says if we are good we shall shine as the stars. [Show star cracker.] Now repeat with me, "Shine as the stars for ever and ever." Now, you see this cross cracker looks bad because the name is broken out. We must never lose the name of Jesus from our hearts. And this heart cracker has no name. Could we stamp a name on it now? "No; it would break." How sad that any heart should not have a Jesus in it! Christ says that we shall be his in the day that he makes up his jewels. [Show diamond cracker.] Jesus loves those that he saves better than his crown or his throne. They are his jewels. [Incident of the mother of the Gracchi.]

Here beside my desk is a large *calla lily*. For its use see "Seed-Thought for Object-Lessons." In the vase with it are some apple blossoms. With them I can illustrate the fostering care of God over children, bringing them up to manhood But these are severed from the tree and are fading. I might use them to illustrate the fifteenth of John. Trailing over my bay window is an ivy which I might use with the same questions as the lesson on the Vine in "Seed-Thought for Object-Lessons." The plants in my hanging basket and flower pots can be used with the story of "The Atheist and the Flower" in "Stories Represented."

These pictures on my wall—"Bible Trees," Belshazzar's

Feast," "A Flower Scene," "The Key of Promise"—may be used for picture teaching; also, this portfolio of sacred pictures, cut from the illustrated papers of the day. I have not exhausted the list, but have said enough to show how abundant are the objects within reach of every teacher.

Toby Veck listened to the chimes as to a living voice, and little Nell's friend heard whispers in the flames of his forge. Shakspeare heard Ariels in the breeze. To Byron "every mountain top had found a tongue." To Tennyson every tree is a "talking oak." To Longfellow, "the voiceless lips of flowers" are "living preachers." Whittier says that "such music as the woods and streams sang in his ear he sang aloud." The Sunday-school teacher needs this "open eye and ear," that every bell and flame and mountain-top and tree and flower and stream may be interpreted, and their God-sent messages understood. Like the servant of the prophet, if our eyes were opened we should see the mountains and fields full of the messages of God.

To the writers of the Bible the rolling year was full of object-lessons: seed, blooming flowers, harvests, withered leaves, "snow like morsels"—all these gave subjects for spiritual teaching. So relics of history, the serpent in the wilderness, the budding rod, the pillar of cloud and fire, the temple vessels, etc., gave them frequent object-lessons. They found in wayside walls, vineyards, kitchens, shops, and temples, some object on which they could hang the truth. Like them, the teacher should find in the garden, the fields, and the home, object-lessons for his work. For young scholars and infant departments especially objects are invaluable. There should be a box or drawer somewhere in connection with the school in which missionary relics, historic trophies, and any object that can be used as an object-lesson, may be kept, new ones being constantly added. And yet the best object-lessons will be those that are fresh and suggested by the present need.

5. *How shall object-lessons be prepared and taught?* In

answering this most important question there are three suggestions for the preparation and four for the teaching:

PREPARATION: (1.) "Search the Scriptures" by means of the Concordance and other helps for all the Scripture passages that may in any way be connected with the object.

(2.) The attributes and uses of the object should be ascertained by a careful analysis. A teacher who fails to do this may be embarrassed and surprised by unexpected developments at the time of teaching. A true story is told of a Roman Catholic priest, who some years ago entered a pulpit in Germany, carrying in his hand a walnut, his intention being to use it as an illustration of what he was about to say. Holding up the little nut in full view of his crowded audience, he began, in a loud and boasting tone, with, "My hearers, the shell of this nut is tasteless and valueless: that, my friends, was Calvin's Church. The skin of this fruit is nauseous, disagreeable, and worthless: that represents the Lutheran Church. And now I will show you the holy Apostolic Church." Suiting his action to his words, he cracked the nut, and, lo and behold! to his utter chagrin and discomfiture the inside contents were perfectly decayed and rotten.

(3.) Study the analogies between the object shown and the truth to be taught. In 1 Kings xxii, 11, 34, 35, we have the case of an object-lesson that sounded very well, but the analogy failed to hold good. A preacher, using hot and cold air as an illustration, said, "The more you heat the air in a receiver the more room there is to put in more air." Another preacher announced as his text, "Thou makest my feet like hen's feet," and used the analogy of their clinging to the roost to teach the duty of clinging to the cross. Such mistakes may usually be avoided by preparing the lesson before attempting to teach it.

TEACHING: (1.) By means of careful questions get the scholars to mention the qualities of the object as far as they are to be used. A teacher should expect peculiar answers at times, and take them good-naturedly, without being disconcerted. A reverend gentleman was addressing a school recently, and was trying to enforce the idea that the hearts of the little ones were sinful and needed regulating. Taking his watch and holding it up, he said: "Now, here is my watch; suppose it don't keep good time—now goes too fast, and now too slow—what shall I do with it?" "Sell it!" shouted a flaxen-headed youngster.

(2.) Call the attention of the class to the Scripture passages, and have a part of them, at least, memorized.

(3.) By questions and explanations make the analogies between the object and the truth clear, and then remove the object from sight.

Hartley, in his "Pictorial Teaching," gives an amusing example of confounding truth with an illustration. A teacher was one day explaining to a class of girls the nature of faith, and by way of illustration pointed through the window to a boat which could be seen upon the river. "Look," said the teacher, "at that boat. You can see it, can you not?" "Yes," said the scholars. "Well, if I were to tell you that there was a mutton pie in the boat under the seat, would you believe me?" "Certainly we should," they replied. "Well," said the teacher, "that is faith." A short time afterward the teacher was again talking to the children on a similar subject, and, asking the question, "What is faith?" was astonished to hear the reply, "*Faith, teacher, is a mutton pie in a boat.*"

(4.) Impress the truth deeply upon the heart, and always close with personal application and prayer. One should always be careful that the truth shall reach the scholar's thoughts more deeply than the object, the latter ever keeping its place as a forerunner simply, and crying, "The truth that cometh after me is greater than I."

OUR BOY'S KNIFE.—During the autumn Harry and I were in the woods gathering leaves. Needing a knife, I asked Harry for his, in order to see of what sort it was, and at the same time learn the contents of our boy's pocket.

He brought out first a piece of apple, then a top and a few bits of string, several marbles, some nails, chalk, candy, slate-pencils, one or two coppers, a piece of paper carefully wrapped, said to have been a school-girl's note, and, last of all, his knife—an article indispensable to most of us, and for which boys have a special longing. This was its condition.

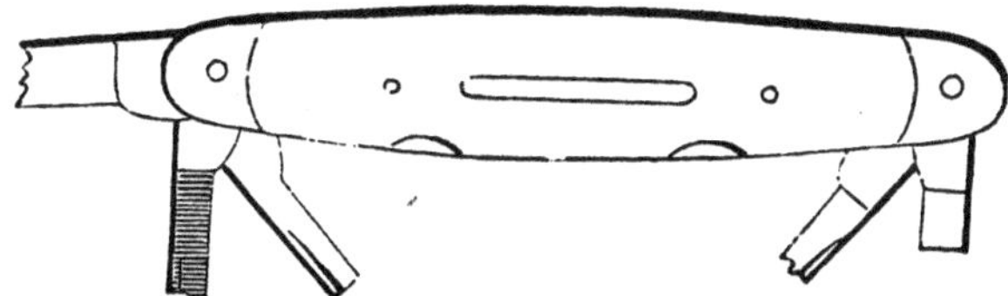

The knife was useless to me, although our boy insisted it answered his purpose *exceedingly* well.

I expressed surprise. Harry confessed that he traded knives, and he could " come it " over the boys first-rate with that knife.

Shortly after I asked Harry if his knife would not be a good text for a sermon. He thought not, but promised to listen attentively to any sermon I might preach from such a text.

On our way home I commenced: First. I am sorry that our boy uses his knife as a means of deception. A lie acted is as great a sin as though spoken; a practice, I regret to say, common to much older boys and many men. Your knife is outwardly attractive. You willfully conceal its imperfections, and thus obtain goods under false pretenses. The same principle was put into practice by the " ring " thieves in New York. Many merchants put false labels on their goods, or cover up the defects of a poor article by a perfect exterior. Any deception acted or spoken is wicked.

" Avoid the least appearance of evil."

Secondly. Your knife is of use only as it is perfect. If nothing but the handle remained it would be an infant's toy. The broken blades are useful for some purposes. Add one or more perfect blades, and it is of greater use. Look at this knife.

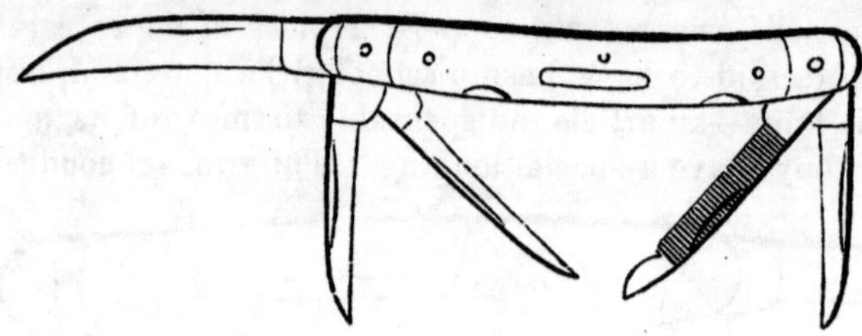

Every blade is sharp, clean, and of a different kind. Thus its capacity for use is great, and remains so in proportion as we keep it in perfect order.

Thirdly. In one sense *we* are knives. The various traits of character we possess are the blades of this human knife, contained in a case which is the body. As knives vary in form and style, so we vary in features and character. As we bring these various traits to perfection, to that degree will we be useful.

Let us consider some traits of character, or blades, which we need in this human knife, for with it we must cut our way through time to eternity.

That you may easily remember, let each letter of the word knife commence the name of these much-needed blades:

K is the blade of KNOWLEDGE. We need knowledge—"knowledge is power." We need to know about God, our Creator. We obtain this from the Bible, which is God's word. It is our chart on this voyage of life. It is the power of God unto our salvation. It contains words of wise counsel. It teaches God's great law of love to him and to our fellows. It contains maxims for every business of life. It tells us how to live, what to live for, and how to secure imperishable riches and an eternal mansion in the skies. We need a knowledge of self, and of the human family; of the world, its history, manners, and customs; of science and philosophy.

N is the NO blade. A small word of vital importance. To learn to use it aright is a hard task. NO at the right time would have saved many a drunkard from hell, made prisons unnecessary, and saved millions of lives and treasure. Always say NO to any promptings of Satan; never to any teachings of God's Holy Spirit.

I is the blade of INDUSTRY—one of the devil's greatest foes. God's plan for man to acquire that which supplies his wants is by WORK. 'Tis industry makes the desert bloom as the rose. It builds cities, spans the world with telegraphs and railroads. One of New York's best merchants remarked, "All that a young man needs in order to succeed is *industry*, economy, and perseverance." He ought to have added something which you will find in the next blade.

F is the blade of FAITH. Faith in God and his word. Faith brings us to the realization of the rich and beautiful promises of the Bible. It makes death a bountiful angel to carry us to a home in heaven. It increases by exercise. We need a faith in self that life will be a success. General Grant's faith conquered rebellion. Professor Morse's faith developed the telegraph. Luther's faith reformed Germany. Read of its mighty triumphs in the eleventh chapter of Hebrews. Embrace the faith there taught. Be watchful that this blade is always sharp, and is never broken.

E is the blade of EXAMPLE. It must be either good or bad. God holds us accountable for its character. "Let your light so shine before men that they may see your good works, and glorify your Father which is in heaven."

Now look at these five blades:

KNOWLEDGE.
NO.
INDUSTRY.
FAITH.
EXAMPLE.

May we possess them all!

V. MAP TEACHING.

Little need be said in regard to the use of maps, as they have been long and widely used in the Sunday-school.

It would be an improvement, perhaps, to the present method of hanging maps, if they were all hung at the most central point for the eyes of the whole school, only one being unrolled at a time, that one, of course, being the one which gives the geography of the lesson. Besides this, every teacher should have a portable Atlas* for his own class. Besides their use for ordinary geographical reference, maps may be used for Bible lectures and reviews. In the latter case, by pointing to the waters, mountains, and towns associated with the last three, or six, or twelve months' study, and asking questions as to the events associated with these geographical points, and giving such explanations as may be required. the facts learned will be strongly impressed on the mind with the help of the eye.

We give the following suggestions for a catechetical and descriptive Bible lecture, with the map of Palestine. Subject: "From Dan to Beersheba." Show the position of "Dan and Beersheba," and also that the expression means the same in regard to Palestine as "from the Atlantic to the Pacific" in regard to the United States. Divide the school, two Sabbaths before the lecture, into three traveling parties, one of them to go from BEERSHEBA to the Mediterranean coast, and then up the coast to Sidon, and across to Dan, studying all incidents of Bible history associated with any of the places through which they would pass, as Gaza, (Samson, Philip,) Joppa, (Peter,) Cæsarea, (Peter, Paul, etc.,) Mount Carmel, (Elijah, Elisha,) Tyre, (Solomon,) Sarepta, (Jesus,) Sidon, Mount Hermon, Damascus, (Paul,) DAN.

* The little pamphlet Atlas published by Nelson & Phillips is one of the very best in quality and variety, and yet is sold at a very low price. These same maps are bound into Whitney's Bible Geography, which should be in every teacher's library as a help to map teaching.

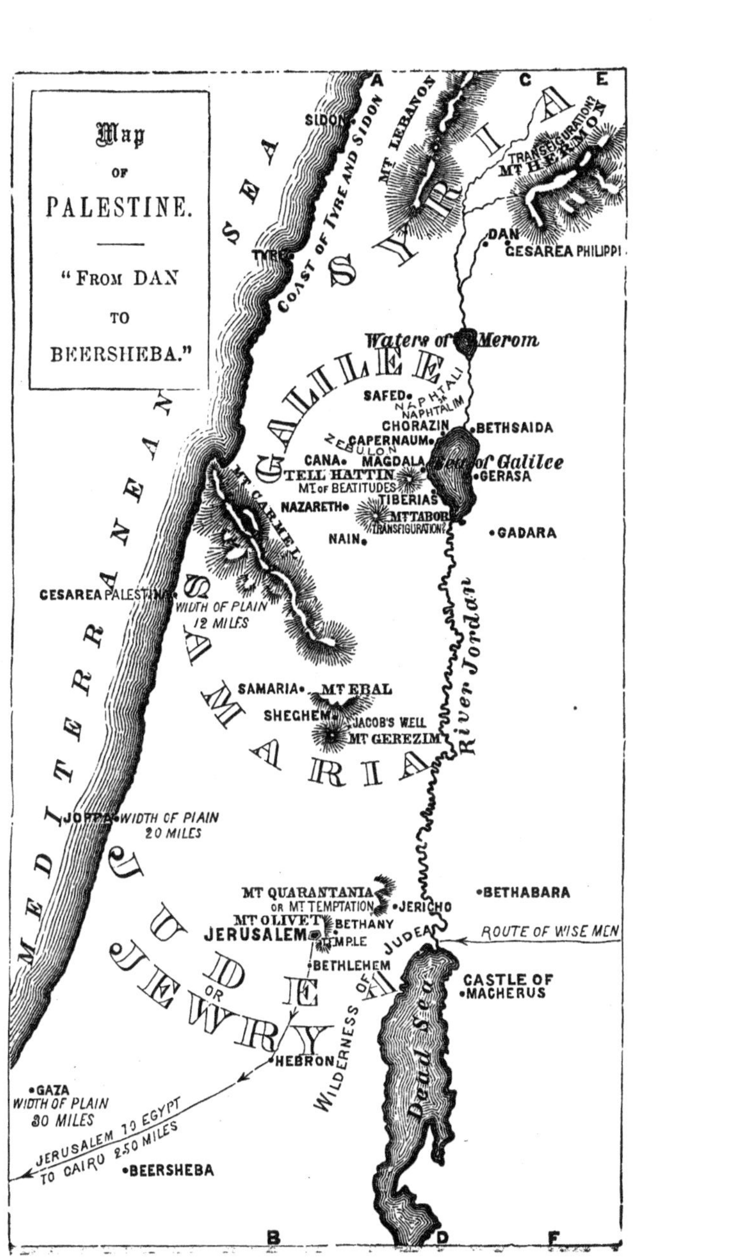
Map of PALESTINE.
"FROM DAN TO BEERSHEBA."
MEDITERRANEAN SEA
SYRIA
GALILEE
SAMARIA
JUDEA OR JEWRY
SIDON
TYRE
COAST OF TYRE AND SIDON
MT LEBANON
MT HERMON
TRANSFIGURATION?
DAN
CESAREA PHILIPPI
Waters of Merom
SAFED
NAPHTALI
NAPHTALIM
CHORAZIN
BETHSAIDA
CAPERNAUM
ZEBULON
CANA
MAGDALA
Sea of Galilee
GERASA
TELL HATTIN
MT OF BEATITUDES
TIBERIAS
NAZARETH
MT TABOR
TRANSFIGURATION?
NAIN
GADARA
MT CARMEL
CESAREA PALESTINA
WIDTH OF PLAIN 12 MILES
River Jordan
SAMARIA
MT EBAL
SHECHEM
JACOB'S WELL
MT GERIZIM
JOPPA
WIDTH OF PLAIN 20 MILES
MT QUARANTANIA OR MT TEMPTATION
JERICHO
BETHABARA
MT OLIVET
BETHANY
JERUSALEM
TEMPLE
BETHLEHEM
ROUTE OF WISE MEN
CASTLE OF MACHERUS
WILDERNESS OF JUDEA
Dead Sea
HEBRON
GAZA
WIDTH OF PLAIN 30 MILES
JERUSALEM TO EGYPT
TO CAIRO 250 MILES
BEERSHEBA
A
B
C
D
E
F

The second party to go from BEERSHEBA across to the Dead Sea, (notice Zoar, Sodom and Gomorrah, Edom, Moab, and Mount Pisgah overlooking the whole;) then up the Jordan (notice its crossing by the Israelites, its waters parted by the prophet's mantle; Jericho, a little way from its banks, whose walls fell, waters were healed, etc., the brook Jabbok that flows into it, Jacob's wrestling-place) to the Sea of Galilee, and coast along its western shore, stopping at Gadara, (demoniac;) then up to the continuation of the Jordan, through to the waters of Merom to Cæsarea Philippi, (Jesus,) and across to DAN.

The third party to go through the center of the country from BEERSHEBA to Hebron, (Abraham,) to Bethlehem, (David, Ruth, Jesus,) to Jerusalem, (see Bible Dictionary, etc.,) to Mount of Olives, (Gethsemane, Ascension, David's retreat, etc.,) to Bethany, (Lazarus, spikenard, etc.,) to Bethel, (Jacob, etc.,) to Gilgal, (Joshua,) to Shechem, (Jacob's well,) stopping to climb Mount Gerizim, (Samaritan temple, blessings and curses,) and Mount Ebal to Samaria, (God's deliverance, etc.;) to Dothan, (Joseph,) to Mount Gilboa, (Saul, etc.,) to Nain, (Jesus,) to Nazareth, (Jesus,) to Cana, (wine,) to Mount Tabor and Mount of Beatitudes; then to the lower part of the Sea of Galilee, and up the eastern coast to Tiberias, (miracles,) Bethsaida, (miracles,) Chorazin, (curses;) then across the sea, recalling the voyages of Christ and his apostles, (the two storms, two draughts of fishes, etc.;) then across the country to DAN.

Teachers and scholars having studied their Bibles and Bible Dictionaries, with their maps, and being prepared to make these three trips, with a knowledge of all the historical associations, the lecturer, with pictures, relics from the East, and incidents from books of travel, can make these journeys very interesting and instructive. A similar lecture can be made with the map of the Israelites' Journey, called "From Rameses to Jerusalem;" and another on the map of the Journeys of St. Paul, called "From Damascus to Rome."

VI. PICTURE TEACHING.

When our parlors are full of Bible pictures, and scarcely a scene in the Bible has not been represented by some master hand, it is strange that Bible pictures have not been used more extensively in Sunday-school teaching. If a school can afford it, the colored pictures on stiff card-board, that are published by our Sunday-School Unions, should be in its "*Cabinet for Eye-Teaching*;" but if there are not means to secure these, a great many pictures may be borrowed from the homes of those in the Church who have well-furnished walls. An infant-class teacher can make even a familiar picture very useful in securing attention. If the lesson be about "Christ in the Manger," one of the many pictures of that scene will afford the best means of making the lesson clear. In almost every community pictures may be found of the leading events of Bible history.*

Besides this, every teacher should have his own Picture Scrap-Book. The illustrated papers will frequently give a picture that may be used some time to illustrate Bible truth. One teacher writes thus to the "Sunday-School Journal:"

"I have a scrap-book in which I am collecting pictures illustrative of the Bible. I buy up every engraving of every sort by which any fact or custom of the Bible may be illus-

* In the Y. M. C. A. at New York a room has been fitted up, called the Sunday-School Exchange, in which may be found a reference library of all the best works published on the Sunday-school cause, which teachers are free to come and consult. All Sunday-school periodicals are also kept on file; also a stock of pictures, maps, and objects suitable for illustrating the Bible have been collected, any of which the teacher may have the privilege of renting.

One of the very best, and by far the cheapest, of helps for picture teaching is the "Bible Roll," by Samuel W. Clark. (Published by Nelson & Phillips.) It comprises twenty-five large views of the tabernacle, temple, Eastern manners, customs, etc. The costumes of the priests, the altars, tables, vails, and other parts of the great symbolic tabernacle, are clearly represented. A school cannot spend five dollars in pictures to better advantage than in securing this valuable collection.

trated. I find Nelson's cards of great value. Already my scrap-book is an attraction to old and young. I hold an occasional 'tea-table talk' with my Sunday scholars as my guests, and the scrap-book makes the time fly. Several times I have taken it with me for use in my class. No trouble to 'get the attention' of my scholars."

It is exceedingly important that the pictures used in Sunday-school teaching should give correct impressions. We have heard of a picture which represents David in his conflict with Goliath, as a young man with his hair parted in the middle! "That, we presume, was to balance him for throwing the stone!"*

A child seeing a picture of the ark which had several windows, exclaimed, "Why, the Bible says there was only *one* window!"

A story is told of two Scotch lads who knew little of gunnery and natural history, but were familiar with King James's Bible and with the winged heads that pass for cherubs in painting and sculpture. Going out a gunning together, one of them shot a bird, and the other ran to secure the trophy. Coming near where it had fallen, he found a white owl so sprawled in the grass as to present to his view only a head with staring eyes and a pair of wings attached. Instantly he shouted in dismay: "Ye're in for it now, Jock, ye've shot a cherubim!"

Correct pictures will be found the clearest and most popular commentaries on many passages of the Bible,† but incorrect pictures are much worse than none.

* M. C. Hazard.

† The most valuable and attractive pictures that can be obtained for use in the Sunday-school or Church are the "large colored diagrams" rented and sold by Nelson & Phillips, and the Depositories of the American Sunday-School Union. The sets of especial value for the lessons of 1877 are. "20. Life and Labors of the Apostle Paul;" "16. Palestine and its Cities;" "17. Mountains of the Bible;" "18. Types of Scripture;" "11 and 12. Fulfilled Prophecy;" "8. Literary History of the Bible;" etc., etc. A set is rented for a Sunday for $1 50. Send for a catalogue.

VII. THE USE AND ABUSE OF THE BLACKBOARD.*

WHAT'S THE USE?

.s the question that rises to many lips when the blackboard is mentioned. It is at once classed by some among the ingenious works of magic, and considered as an eccentric intruder among the helps to religious teaching. In order to answer this question, "What's the use?" let us prefix two letters to the last word and notice a preliminary question:—

WHAT'S THE ABUSE?

One who is well known in the Sunday-school work writes these well-timed words on the abuse of the blackboard: "I am fully conscious, as all who have thoughtfully observed the course of this line of teaching, I think, must be, that it has been made the victim of most absurd exaggerations and complicated follies. Intended to be *the simplest*, *the clearest*, and *the most vivid of methods*, it has been made by a large class of blackboard delineators a vehicle of the most extravagant imaginations and the most absurdly unimpressive exercises. What I have always pleaded for in its use, and do now more than ever, is pith, point, clearness, conciseness, the latter especially."

The chief abuses of the blackboard cluster around the idea of *making an exhibition of it rather than an illustration by it.* "Truth and art should serve each other; but in the king's palace art must be the servant of his law. When God's law is made the *servant* of art in Sunday-school blackboarding, no wonder honest natures are disgusted."

The blackboard is related to the truth that is to be taught as John the Baptist was related to Christ. It should be only

* All this section equally appropriate to the use of a slate in each Sunday-school class.

"a voice," itself unnoticed while its message fills all hearts, "preparing the way of the Lord." This thought is embodied in decayed sculpture at Melrose Abbey. Above the beautiful stone foliage at the south door is a niche in which an image of Christ formerly stood, and beneath it there is still seen a half-length figure of John the Baptist, looking reverently up to the Master above him, and drawing all other eyes to the same place and away from himself. Under it is written, "*Ecce Filius Dei,*" (Behold the Son of God.) No better representation of the true mission of the blackboard in the Sunday-school could be given. It must point away from itself to Christ; not leading men to say, "How skillful!" or "How beautiful!" but rather, "How true!"*

Mr. Moody once gave a blackboard exercise in California, in which he contrasted in opposite columns

THE WORLD'S GIFTS AND GOD'S GIFTS.

Money.	Jesus.
Houses.	Angels.
Clothes.	Friends.
Honors.	Promises.
Pleasures.	Peace.

The exercise was made so fully a forerunner and herald of Christ that it resulted in the conviction and conversion of an unconverted teacher who was present. Many other conversions have occurred through the spiritual use of the blackboard.

"The use of the blackboard for illustrating Bible truths is

*Be careful always that the full force of the illustration goes to illuminate the truth which you are expounding The foot-lights are studiously vailed from the eyes of the spectators, but they throw a luster on the actor's face. Like them, our illustrations must not draw attention to ourselves, but to the truth we have in hand. We must not turn them on ourselves, but on the Master and his work. It is as criminal to hide him beneath gorgeous illustrations as it is to ignore him altogether. We may and ought to cover our faces before him; but we must never put a vail, no matter how exquisite may be its texture, over his countenance.—*Rev. Wm. M. Taylor, D.D.*

condemned by a few of our best thinkers for its materialistic tendencies. It is urged that the use of material objects for presenting truth leads the mind into the errors of materialism. God did not think so while teaching the Jews the principles of Judaism. He thundered on Sinai that they might HEAR him in his power and wrath; but this was not enough; they had eyes as well as ears, and he *wrote* his laws on leaves of stone that they might SEE him in its truths, and then commanded them to '*write* these words on the posts of their houses, and on their gates.'" *

In the use of the blackboard the same law holds as in the other departments of Church work, "The letter killeth, but the Spirit giveth life."

Another class of blackboard abuses arises from incorrect drawing or incomplete explanation. A superintendent, having drawn what he intended for an *eye* on the blackboard, asked, "Now, what do you see on the board?" A boy answered, "*An oyster shell.*"

One who cannot draw outlines correctly will do the best and safest work by confining himself to lettering. †

Sometimes misapprehensions similar to the one just mentioned occur as much from incomplete explanation as from incorrect drawing, as in the case where a man represented faith by a shield, somewhat resembling a kitchen boiler cover, which was so confusedly explained that one of the scholars, when he was asked, "What is faith?" replied, "A kitchen boiler cover."

Such answers will sometimes be given when the outline is correctly drawn, as the following illustration will show:—

* Rev. J. F. Clymer.

† See "Table of Blackboard Alphabets" in last pages of the book. There are some who secure the benefits of drawing in the presence of the school and avoid the errors of incorrect drawing by making the picture or outline beforehand with soapstone, whose lines can be seen by the speaker, but not by the school, and then at the appropriate time using the chalk rapidly on these lines that are already faintly drawn.

Says J. S. Ostrander, "Not a great while ago I was present at a large Sunday-school meeting, in which one of our most successful teachers used the board to illustrate the idea of a sacrifice. He drew an altar, and upon it a lamb, around which he drew, with *red crayon*, representations of the consuming fire. The whole was well done. The children were pleased and instructed. 'What is this, children?' he said, pointing to the altar, lamb, etc., to all of which correct answers were obtained. Finally the simplicity and innocence of a little child was discovered by the putting of the following question by the speaker: "And what is this? (pointing to the *red chalk representation of fire.*) After some hesitancy a little voice in the congregation responded, '*I guess they are the feathers of the lamb.*' Like a good questioner, the brother received the answer with respect, and proceeded to 'simplify and repeat.'"

Yet another class of abuses may be included under the term, "complicated follies and false emphasis." Here are several published specimens:

The Leader's parting woRD
The vow the big stone heaRD
It and the writing plAIN
In law-book, still remAIN
Teaching when Joshua's dEAD
That God is Israel's hEAD

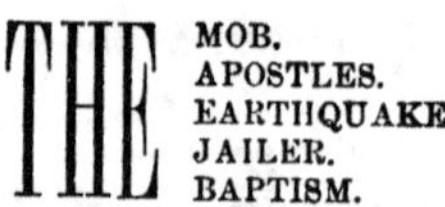

An advertiser tries the mystifying blackboard spelling in announcing his wares, after this fashion:—

VA LE/R N TIN/ISH E'S.

Some anonymous writer tries it on the history of Henry VIII.:

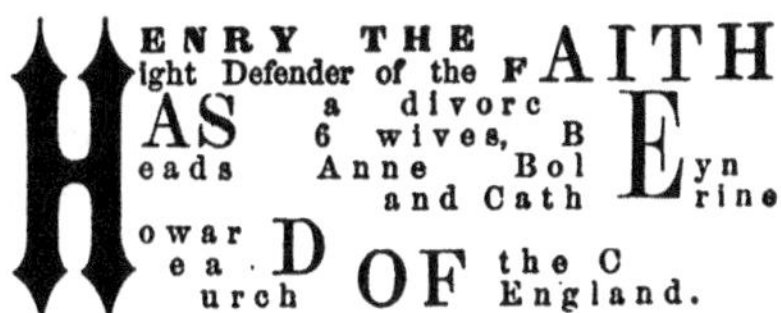

The query with which the last-named writer heads his exposure of such complicated follies is fitly chosen:

W I OR HA T ?

Apply this question to the following exercises on David and Goliath:

THE P

HILISTINE CHAMPION.
USILLANIMOUS ISRAELITES.
LUCKY SHEPHERD-BOY.
ONDEROUS ARMOR.
ICKED-
EBBLES.
ROUD GOLIATH.
IOUS DAVID.
ROVOKED GIANT.
ROPHESYING LAD.
ROMPT ATTACK.
RONE PHILISTINE.
REVAILING CHAMPION.
ENETRATING SWORD.
ARTED HEAD-AND-BODY
ANIC STRICKEN HOST.
ÆANS OF VICTORY.

The "Sunday-School Times," commenting on this subject editorially, utters these well-timed words:

"The real worth of an outline is as a helpful and instructive analysis. If it does not serve in that direction it is useless. It may, to be sure, be *more easily fixed in the memory* through an acrostic, or an alliteration; but of what use is its memorizing when to begin with it is good for nothing?

"*The true test, then, of a suggested outline of any Bible lesson, or other statement of truth, is in its value apart from its alliterative or acrostical structure.* If the outline does not prove to be a good one when words of a similar meaning beginning with different letters are substituted for those suggested in the fanciful plan, the outline is worthless in spite of all the ingenuity displayed in its arrangement. For example, if the lesson were the story of David and Goliath, it might be well to consider the narrative in study or teaching under the natural divisions of, 1. Goliath's challenge to the Israelites; 2. Their fear of meeting him; 3. David's trustful acceptance of the challenge; 4. The ensuing fight; 5. Its issue. This outline might be stated as an aid in securing attention, or in memorizing the divisions:

THE C HALLENGE BY GOLIATH.
OWARDICE OF ISRAEL.
OURAGE OF DAVID.
ONFLICT OF CHAMPIONS.
OMPLETE VICTORY.

This outline is certainly quite as good without the alliteration as with it. Many sensible teachers would prefer to use it in the less fanciful form, while others would find it practically more helpful in its alliterative statement. In this case the outline is first secured; then the alliteration is sought. A more common way with blackboardists seems to be to pick out a letter and see how many phrases ingeniously drawn from the lesson may be strung on it."

The rule in blackboard lettering should be, *As large letters give emphasis and prominence, they should never be used except where they make up an important syllable or word or phrase that needs to be emphasized, or when they may legitimately help the memory in an initial or acrostic exercise without destroying the logical outline of the lesson.*

[Erasing "Ab," and leaving the question as at first, "What's the use?"]

Let us now notice the simple and practical uses of the Sunday-school blackboard:

By printing this brief word any one can collect the attention of an audience in a moment, or by simply raising a piece of chalk to the blackboard without making even so much as a dot.

1. The first use of the blackboard, then, is

TO COLLECT ATTENTION.

A lady unfriendly to the Sunday-school said to a little girl who attended it, "Do you have to pay any thing at Sunday-school?" The child answered, "No—yes, we do; we have to *pay attention*." This Sunday-school tax of attention is one of the hardest taxes to collect, but it can be quickly and effectually done by the simplest touch of the chalk to the blackboard.

In Congress or Parliament it is an important thing to "catch the eye" of the presiding officer at the right moment. The ingenuous and varied signs along the street, above the stores, are also earnest efforts to "catch the public eye." The blackboard accomplishes this in religious teaching.

Its power to attract attention may be easily verified by taking up a newspaper and finding what style of advertisements first arrest the eye. *It will be those most resembling the blackboard.* So also of advertisements on rocks and fences.

2. The Rev. Geo. A. Peltz recommends the use of

THE BLACKBOARD AS A BULLETIN.

"Use it for special announcements. Much time is unnecessarily wasted in calling attention to the various matters connected with the economy of the school. The proper use of the blackboard here will greatly aid order and quiet. For example, how suggestive would be the display of a board neatly lettered, as follows:

NEXT SUNDAY

MISSIONARY COLLECTION

FOR

HEATHEN LANDS.

FREELY GIVE! FREELY GIVE!

3. A third use of the blackboard is

TO AID THE MEMORY.

Three words represent the laws of successful memorizing—*interest*, *attention*, *exercise*. All these laws are pre-eminently fulfilled in blackboard illustration. When a pastor or superintendent lifts the chalk to the blackboard interest is awakened, attention is secured, and the mind is exercised in curiosity as to what is coming next,* and what is to be the meaning of the completed work. Each word written on the blackboard is written at the same moment upon the memory of those who follow the movements of the chalk.

Like the new "letter writer," the blackboard allows us to write many duplicate copies of our message at once, as many as there are minds present. A symbol or picture drawn upon the blackboard is drawn also at the same time upon the memories of all who are following the artist; so that from the blackboard as a negative, copies are printed upon every mind. Tyndall once said that were he lecturing on gravitation, and should say to his hearers, "I hold a marble in my hand, and were I to release it the power of gravitation would instantly draw it to the earth," he would not feel that he had produced the desired impression upon his auditors until he had actually permitted the marble to fall to the floor, and thus availed himself of the co-operation of the senses in immediate connection with the definition of science, for the purpose of stamping its impress indelibly upon the memory of the

* The point here hinted at is the chief objection to the new plan of stenciling letters on the blackboard by pulverizing chalk and using it as ink is ordinarily used with stencils. This plan would afford more perfect letters than are usually formed on blackboards; but, as the stenciling would need to be done before the school session opened, this memory law of *exercise* and *curiosity* would have to be sacrificed, and the loss would be more than the gain. However, in such elaborate exercises as must be put on in advance, which should be much less frequent than exercises wrought out before the eyes of the school, the stencil might profitably be used by those who have no skill in lettering.

audience. Even spoken illustrations or word-pictures show this same quality in a less degree. Dr. Guthrie, in his early ministry, held a Bible-class of young people on Sabbath evenings, in which he spoke more illustratively of Christian truth than he felt at liberty to do in preaching.

He soon found that these informal and illustrated talks were much better remembered than his less illustrated sermons, and that the people remembered best the truths that were pictured in an illustration. From this experience he was led to use illustrations far more abundantly in preaching and writing, and made himself one of the most popular and successful of preachers and authors.*

When the picture summoned before the eye is not imaginary, but real, the impression on the memory is much stronger, and hence blackboard illustration becomes the king of mnemonic helps.

FORGET NOT ALL HIS BENEFITS.

Forget that sentence if you can.

4. Another simple use of the blackboard is

TO EXPLAIN THE TRUTH.

A Sunday-school had been studying the parable of the two houses, one built on the rock and the other on the sand. Most of the scholars were familiar with the story, but had not realized it. The outline of the two houses was then put before the eyes of the school and the parable was then explained. A thrill of new interest was felt, and one expressed the feelings of all when he whispered, "O, I see!"

When a general is mapping out a campaign he draws his

* By awakening and gratifying the imagination the truth finds its way more readily to the heart and makes a deeper impression on the memory. The story, like a float, keeps it from sinking; like a nail, fastens it to the mind; like the feathers of an arrow, makes it strike; and, like the barb, makes it stick.—*Guthrie.*

plans and locates his armies by pins. When an architect wants to explain a building his pencil and paper do most of the talking. In a village in India, it became necessary in the course of some engineering operations to transport an enormous mass of metal, weighing several hundred tons, from one part of the town to another. Ordinary means were out of the question; and as the engineers found themselves unable to devise any process, they did the next best thing, and wrote to other engineers in England, who were constantly supervising such work. The latter, instead of writing out nice large pages of foolscap, beautifully embellished with Greek letter *formulæ* and red ink, quietly waited until the next big piece of metal which they had to transport offered a favorable opportunity. Then they prepared a camera, and photographed every step of the operation, together with all the tools and appurtenances, and forwarded the prints from the negatives to India. These the engineers in the far-off country followed, and with little difficulty accomplished their task. The blackboard may be used with like helpfulness in the Christian warfare, and in the building of character to explain the unknown.

Take the parable of the sower. To represent the different fields in which the seed (the word of God) is sown by the sower, (the Christian,) draw first the outline of *an ear* for the wayside. Below it write the fate of the seed—"Devoured." Above write the name of the devourer, "Satan." Then draw two distorted and shriveled hearts. On one write "Stony;" below it, "Withered;" above it, "Weak Faith." On the other write "Thorns;" below it, "Choked;" above it, "Temptation." Then draw a full heart, and write on it "Good Ground;" above it write "The Holy Spirit," and below, "Received the Seed," "Bore much Fruit."

"If your lesson is on the 'Gadarene Demoniac,' draw an ancient tomb with a broken chain beside it. If on the 'Ten Virgins,' draw ten lamps, five burning, and five gone out. If on death, natural or spiritual, draw two or three graves. If on 'Christ, the Light of the World,' draw the rising sun shining upon a house with closed blinds. Such parables as 'The Builders,' 'The Friend at Midnight,' and some others, suggest their own pictures. The cave where Elijah heard the still small voice may be represented by a dark spot looking like a cave on the side of a mountain.

A striking instance of the value of the blackboard as a means of explanation was seen in the lesson on Gideon's Victory, prepared by the famous war correspondent of the "Boston Journal," Mr. C. "Carleton" Coffin, for the "Congregationalist" in 1875, in which he introduced a map of the scene that was self-explanatory, and showed more to the

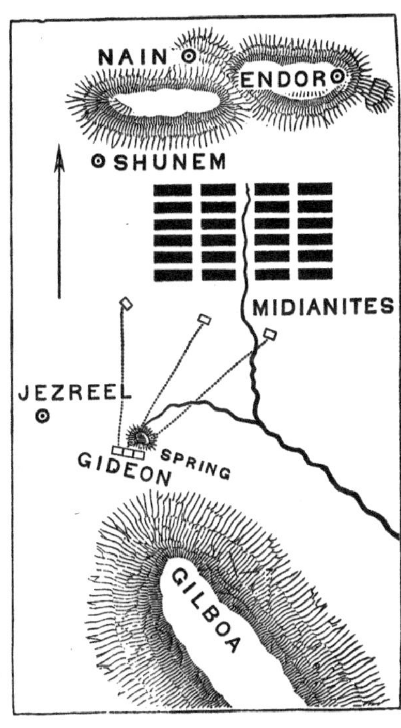

eye in a moment than an hour's teaching could have shown through the ear. Most lessons might be thus lighted up and explained by using the blackboard or slate, presenting a map of the scene or some other exercise.

A very interesting lesson may be made from the 'Mustard Seed' by drawing in colors a tree, full size (enlarge from Bible dictionary) of the mustard-tree, and by its side a dot, representing the seed. An old-fashioned well on one side, on the other the name 'Jesus,' may furnish an introduction to a talk about the 'Living Water,' and so on indefinitely."

When the eastern plow, or the stones with which grinding was done, or the altar, or candlestick, or any other articles of household or temple use are mentioned, whose outlines are simple, they will be better understood than by any word description if a Bible dictionary is examined and the outline is sketched on the board.

5. Another practical use of the blackboard is

TO CONDENSE THOUGHT.

When we wish a message or resolution condensed into the fewest possible words, we say, "Please put it in writing." When we send messages by telegraph, knowing that there is an extra charge for more than ten words, we learn how much can be said in ten words. "Blackboarding" is Sunday-school telegraphy, the blackboard being the battery, the crayon the key. One who uses the blackboard learns to put outlines, facts, and thoughts in the briefest and fewest words. How impressive (more than any longer message could have been) was that telegram, sent by a man who had escaped from the wreck of the *Atlantic*, near Halifax, to his partner at New York:

A contrast is to be expressed between good and evil, or between joy and sorrow. Half an hour would do it in spoken words; put them in opposite colors or positions on the black board and the contrast is at once apparent. A wrong idea is to be presented and overthrown. How much a long argument may be condensed by writing the wrong idea upon the blackboard, and then destroying it with the eraser to make room for writing the truth, or by canceling it with the truth written over it!

In the story of the feeding of the five thousand, the word translated "ranks" means, in some cases, flower-beds. This suggests a concise picture of God's care over us, as follows (remembering that "they sat down in ranks, by hundreds, and by fifties"):

God's Garden.

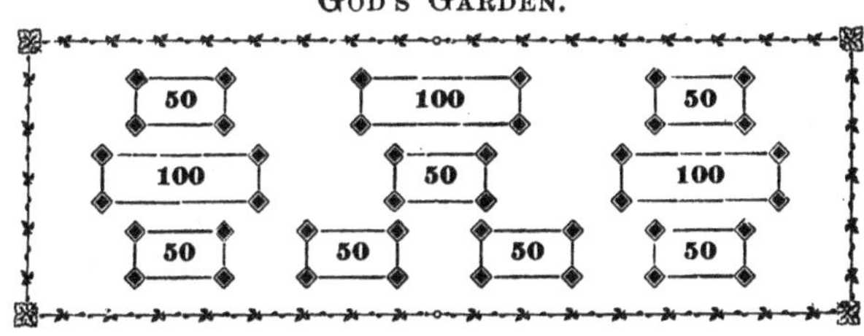

6. Another simple use of the blackboard is

TO EMPHASIZE TRUTH.

God might have sent a spoken message to Belshazzar by the lips of Daniel, but was it not more terribly impressive when the letters of fire flashed upon the king's eyes from the wall:

"MENE, MENE, TEKEL, UPHARSIN?"

With a palace wall as a blackboard and crayons of fire the divine hand inscribed the king's death-warrant. The philosophy is the same on which the blackboard teaching of to-day is based.

In what essential particular does the Divine teacher's method of instructing Peter in a world embracing charity by a vision-sheet full of beasts, differ from a Christian superintendent's method of impressing his school by some simple symbolical outline on the blackboard? What message of Christ was more impressive or successful than the unknown words he wrote on the ground, with the sand for his blackboard and his finger for a crayon? Before the power of that eye-sermon in the sand his whole audience of hypocrites fled away.

There is a great emphasis in putting the truth, whether on board or paper, "down in black and white."

"BEHOLD, I STAND AT THE DOOR AND

KNOCK!"

This message will be photographed in an instant upon the heart and memory, and cannot be forgotten.

Various degrees of emphasis are indicated by the *size* and *position* of words. A word in large capitals or a word having a whole line is made especially emphatic, as seen in the following:

WHATSOEVER

THE LORD

HATH SAID UNTO

THEE,

DO?

"Whatsoever," "thee," and "do," are made emphatic by *position;* "the Lord," by *size* of letters.

Emphasis, with pleasing variety, also, may be secured by the judicious use of colored crayons. While yellow and white are the only colors that are clear and distinct when used alone, every color may be brought out by making *block letters*, in which two colors are used in appropriate combinations, as blue with white, yellow with green, blue with light brown, blue with red, and in general a light color with a dark one. Several patterns of block letters will be found in the "Table of Blackboard Alphabets" in the last pages of the book.

7. Another practical use of the blackboard is to

REVIEW THE LESSONS,

to draw from the scholars the information already imparted to them by their teachers. In most cases the exercise should not be written or printed on the blackboard before the time when it is to be used, except, perhaps, a few catch-words and initials. Questions should then be asked, and the answers briefly indicated with the chalk, until the exercise is complete. Lines, dots, and letters will often be sufficient to hold the attention and impress the thought. Difficult exercises must generally be made before the school-session; but all that can be drawn from the scholars by questions, and readily delineated or printed, should be left to the time of using the exercise. This will allow one to take advantage of curiosity, which loves to witness the creation of a thing.

In an acrostic exercise, the acrostic letters may sometimes be put on beforehand; in a table exercise, the outline of the table; in a canceling or erasing exercise, that which is to be canceled or erased; in a map exercise, the simple outline without the points of interest indicated.

In this book the exercises are usually given as they would appear when completed. It is intended that each exercise should be developed, by questions, point by point. The following

REVIEW OF THE LIFE OF CHRIST,

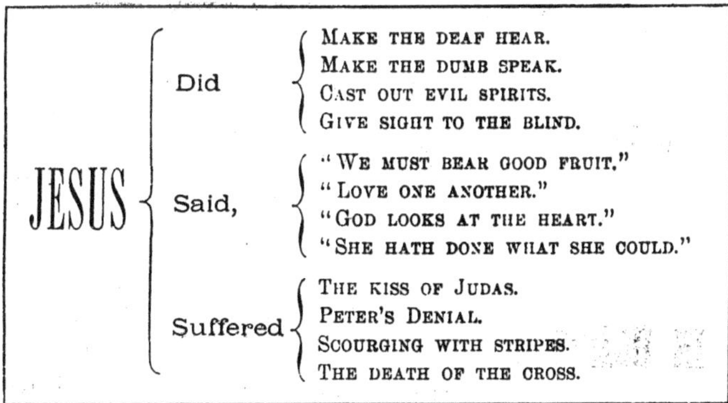

taken from the "Sunday-School Chronicle," will show the development of a blackboard exercise. The process would be essentially the same for the review of one lesson, or a month's work as for a quarter's, as in this case. First, the superintendent asks, "About whom have we been studying these three months?" He prints the answer, "Jesus." Then he says, "We want to recall what he 'did,' what he 'said,' and what he 'suffered.'" Accordingly he prints these three words in the relative positions indicated. "Now, what did Christ 'DO' in the lessons we have studied?" From one and another the various answers come, helped, perhaps, by a hint or two from the superintendent. "Now, what were some of the sweetest things that Jesus 'SAID' in these lessons?" The answers are epitomized into the fewest words on the blackboard. So also with the third point. Each answer under all three points is explained, illustrated, and enforced, and appropriate songs are interspersed to vary the exercise.

The method of conducting the blackboard reviews of single lessons may be illustrated by the following on the lesson of "Paul and Silas in Prison," Acts xvi, 22–34. [Unless a blackboard is very large both sides will be needed for this exercise:]

GOD SAVES

IN HOMEFULS. {
NOAH—"Come thou and thy
ABRAHAM—"Teach his
JOSHUA—"As for me and my
JAILER—"Saved, and thy
} HOUSE."

BY { SONG —Johoshaphat.
—Paul and Silas.
—The Reformers.
PRAYER —"Lord save me."
—"Revive thy work." }

What must I do?

1. Do thyself no harm by rejecting
2. Believe on the Lord Jesus
3. Sing, pray, work, for

CHRIST.

At the beginning of the review nothing is upon the board except the words, "God saves," "From," "In," "By." The superintendent says, "In this lesson we see God's power to save both his followers and his enemies. What did God save his apostles from?" "Yes, from prison, or in general, from 'peril.'" (Prints it.) "Mention some other instances in which God rescued his people." The answers include "Israel in Egypt," "Daniel," "Three worthies." These, with "apostles," are written as indicated. The superintendent impresses the thought of God's care and power to help. "But God saved some in that prison who were not his followers. Who? From what?" "Yes, from 'sin.' (Writes,) Who else does God save from 'sin?' (Writes reply,) All who believe in Christ." Illustrates what it is to believe in Christ. "Was any one saved from sin but the jailer?" "Yes, God saved a *homeful*, as he has done so often in Christian history." (Write "homefuls.") "Now mention some other cases in the Bible where a whole household served the Lord." The cases of "Noah," "Abraham," and "Joshua," are mentioned, and with the "jailer" are written on the blackboard with the indicated texts. The superintendent asks, "What means that were used in the prison does God often use to save men?" Writes down the answers, "Song," "Prayer." The case of Jehoshaphat and the songs of the Reformation are used as illustration and noted on the blackboard. "What two kinds of prayers are we to use?" (For ourselves and for others.) "I will write one of each." (Writes, "Lord, save me," and "Revive thy work.") "Now comes the practical question for us, as well as the jailer, What must I do?" The three points are written, then emphasized and illustrated for both Christians and the unconverted. The blackboard is especially valuable for Quarterly Reviews. The most satisfactory plan we have known to be successfully and continuously employed is one originated by Rev. J. H. Vincent, and used in the Plainfield (N. J.) Methodist Episcopal Sunday-school, James M'Gee, superintendent. A large sheet of *lapinum*, or blackboard cloth, about nine feet by four, has been nailed to the wall, back of the desk, at a cost of less than ten dollars, and set apart wholly to the Quarterly Review, leaving the other blackboard of the school for other use. This blackboard cloth has been ruled, as on the following page. The top column across the page contains the number of the quarter and the numbers of the lessons from I to XII. The first column down the page indicates the points in each lesson that are to be reviewed.

In the second column down the page we see the application of this plan to the first lesson of the third quarter of 1876, as found in the "Berean Question Book." The explanation of this column will show the application of the plan for any lesson and with any question book or lesson leaf. The question is asked, "What is the title of the lesson?" The answer is given by the school, "David's charge to Solomon," which is indicated on the blackboard only in initials as a help to memory, "D. C. S." Then the question in regard to topic is answered, "Ministry to God divinely appointed," which is epitomized in the letters, "M. G. D. A." The golden text, "Know thou the God of thy father, etc.," is indicated by its first word. The outline, "MINISTRY TO GOD APPOINTED"—

1. As to what men shall do;
2. As to how men shall do,

THIRD QUARTER.	I.	II.	III.	IV.	V.	VI.	VII.	VIII.	IX.	X.	XI.	XII.
Titles, - - -	D. C. S.	S. C.										
Topics or Central Thoughts, -	M.G.D.A.	M.G.O.W.										
Golden Texts, -	"Know-	"If any-										
Outline, - -	M. G. A. Wh. How.	R. O. G. O. W. C. O. B.										
Doctrine, - -	G. S.	F. A. M.										
Extra Drill, -												

is repeated and epitomized in the same way, and also the "doctrine" of the lesson, "God a sovereign." A few moments are given to some extra drill on the Catechism, the books of the Bible, or some other subject, for which the remaining column is used. The other blackboards are used for pictorial or other exercises on each lesson in addition to this memory drill.

On the second Sunday the second lesson is developed in the same manner, and the first is reviewed. This review of all the preceding lessons of the quarter occurs every Sunday after the drill on the new lesson, and is necessary to a thorough Quarterly Review.

To give variety in the appearance of the exercise, on some quarters, twelve books are represented as standing on a shelf, and the initials as above are put on their backs, each book representing a lesson.

Twelve picture frames might be drawn for a still further change, or a pillar with twelve stones, or a road with twelve milestones, the details being essentially the same in each case.

The blackboard, then, is of great value in the Sunday-school for winning attention, helping memory, making announcements, explaining truth, condensing thought, emphasizing ideas, and reviewing lessons.

What to Take Out of a Lesson for the Blackboard.

Those who are unaccustomed to the use of the blackboard may not know at first what should be taken out of a lesson and put before the eye. The parts to be thus used are usually either the central thought, the Golden Text, the great doctrine, the prominent duty, the outline, or the warning, of the lesson. When "what to use" has been searched out, then the "how to use it" should be considered,—whether to make it an outline picture, or an acrostic, or what form will best emphasize the point to be taught, explain its meaning, and impress it on the memory, with due regard also to pleasing variety.

MATERIALS WANTED.

A large revolving blackboard is, of course, the best.* It affords a great advantage in that the exercise on one surface may front the school during the lesson, and another exercise may be held in reserve on the hidden side for the closing review. Often it is well to have a simple exercise on the front, such as a motto, or a word exercise; a symbol exercise or outline exercise being kept on the reverse side until the other has been used. Some carpenter interested in the school will sometimes make such a blackboard at a low price, but its great usefulness will be an ample reward for an extra effort to obtain it. Those who are building new churches should put in a fine wall blackboard. If neither of these can be had, a poor one is far better than none. Then a good eraser, a long, stout rule, a good pointer, and a box of mixed crayons, will make an outfit. White crayons should generally be used, but other colors sometimes add greatly to the variety and strength of expression. By gaslight yellow crayons are most distinct. Use round chalk for writing, square chalk for printing. "Bear on! Speak loud to the eye!" A free and off-hand way of writing and printing should be cultivated.

The blackboard excels nearly all other forms of illustration in convenience, availability, and cheapness. Description and allegories require more time to reach the heart through the ear than the blackboard to reach it through the eye. "Objects" for object lessons are shown but once, while the blackboard may be used again and again for an indefinite time. Pictures have one unchanging surface, while the blackboard gives opportunity for fresh and varied illustrations. Maps are purchased at considerable expense, and many schools cannot supply themselves with a sufficient number for a thorough

*By far the cheapest method of getting a blackboard is to buy one or two yards of "Blackboard Cloth," for one or two dollars, and hang it upon the wall or nail it upon an easel. Many prefer it even to the best blackboards. It is manufactured by "The Silicate Slate Company," corner of Church and Fulton Streets, New York, and sold by many book-sellers.

study of Bible geography. Blackboard maps may present the towns, rivers, and mountains mentioned in the lesson more prominently than any published maps would do it.

How to Make Letters.*

"The plainest letter is generally the best, and one of the easiest styles of letter to make is called the block letter.

"*How are they made?* If the word or sentence is to be written on a straight line, place the ruler against the board, and draw the crayon faintly on each side of it; that will make two parallel lines three inches apart, thus:

"Next, lower the rule, say three fourths of an inch, and rule again, thus:

"The upper and lower spaces enable you to make the top and bottom of the lines even and of the same size.

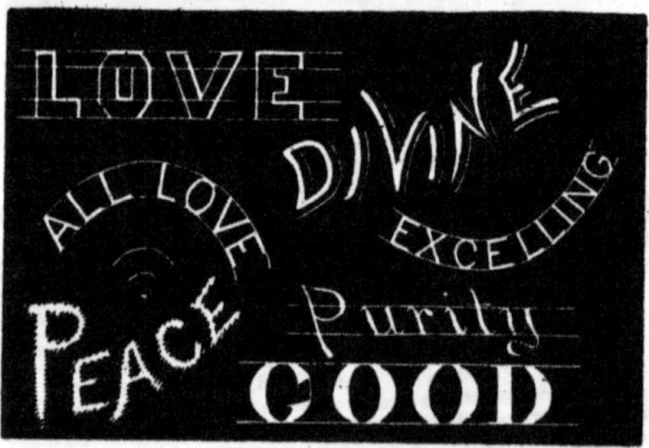

"Say the word to be written is **L-O-V-E.** Remember that the parallel lines just ruled always make the top and bottom of the letters, and to complete them the down lines only have to be made.

"See diagram. The

*For further varieties of letters see "Table of Blackboard Alphabets" in closing pages of the book.

Charles B. Stout says that a blackboard should not be black at all. "Boards colored a sea-green," he says, "are very agreeable to the eye, and afford a fine ground for chalk and crayon. On boards of a delicate sky-blue the chalk shines with almost dazzling whiteness."

Manufacturers of blackboards say that while this is so when a *blueboard* is new, it soon becomes blurred, and is then less distinct than the black. If one should use the blue it would doubtless be necessary to wash it before each use, and frequently renew the liquid slating or coloring.

heavy lines show the down lines. Letters made with one colored crayon and shaded with that of another color are very prominent; for instance, a yellow letter shaded with red. Be careful to make the shading on the same side of each letter.

"Another way to make showy letters is to make them regardless of proportion, in all sorts of irregular shapes; see the word *Divine* in the diagram. The letters look best shaded.

"To write words in a semicircle, make guiding lines by fastening a piece of crayon to the string; with the left hand hold the string against the board, and with the right hand describe the circle. (See diagram on p. 72.)

"Broad letters made with the side of the crayon show well. See the word *Peace.*

"Letters written as in the word *Purity* are not difficult to make.

"Use the string in making letters with curved lines. See the word *Good.*

"A bold, vigorous stroke always looks better than a weak, timid one, even though not so true." *

"Any man who has influence enough to receive the votes of any company of men and women to be the superintendent of their Sabbath-school has *ability* to use the blackboard if he only has *willingness* to use it in this simple, unostentatious way.

"The plainest sort of a man, with the lesson in his head and heart, baptized with the spirit of self-forgetfulness, whose only aim is to impress God's truth on youthful hearts, will do more with his rudest chalkings than the skillful blackboardist with his perfect diagrams, but without his Christly spirit and aim.

"Here, at least, *heart* is greater than *art.*" †

THE SLATE.

To the individual teacher the slate is as helpful as the blackboard to the pastor or superintendent. All that may be

* J. B. Phipps, in "The Normal Class." † Rev. J. F. Clymer.

said of the advantages of the blackboard to the school may be said of the slate in regard to the class. Every teacher who can write a plain hand, even though unskillful with the pencil, may use the slate with great profit.

If the lesson is descriptive, make a frame by drawing four lines, and then put within it the objects mentioned in the lesson—straight marks for people, squares for houses, crosses for trees, and acute angles for mountains. These, with the imagination of the class, will make a picture which will fix a lesson in the mind so that it will never be forgotten.

It would be a profitable investment for a Sunday-school to buy for all its teachers silicate slates large enough to give a foot square of surface when opened, and have the superintendent in the teachers' meetings suggest maps, outlines, etc., for the teachers to use on their slates in their classes, in addition to what might be held in reserve for the general blackboard.

The blackboard exercises given in this book may be used with equal appropriateness on a teacher's slate.

Every scholar also should have a slate to make a map of the scene of the lesson, written answers to special questions given out on the previous Sunday, written epitomes of the home readings or some other part of the lesson, etc.

A Classification

of blackboard exercises will now follow, arranged in a natural order from the simplest to the most difficult, from the simplest motto to the more elaborate outline exercise. Enough are given under each class to show distinctly what we mean by its name and to suggest many others.

1. The Motto Exercise.—The simplest form of black-

board exercise is to write or print the Golden Text, or a religious precept or proverb, or some motto or watchword, on the blackboard. By breaking it up into short lines, emphasizing important words by colors, large capitals, and a position by themselves, such mottoes are often made very impressive. The following is a good illustration of the arrangement of a motto on the blackboard:

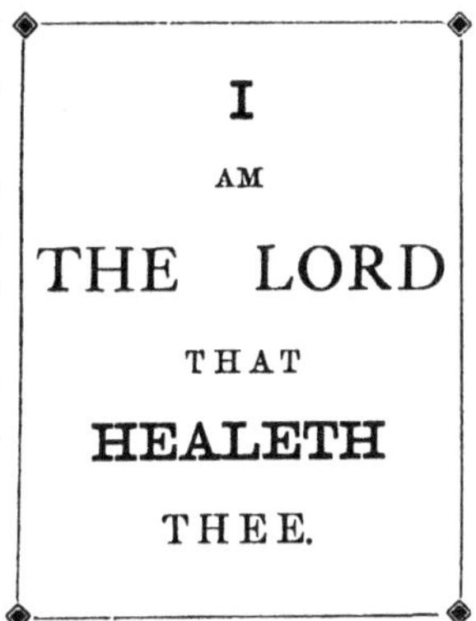

"The Lord" "healeth" "thee" stand out prominent, both on account of position and size. "Healeth" should be in red, to suggest the cleansing blood, and "thee" in white, to represent "white as snow."

Even the writing of a simple precept on the blackboard about which you wish to speak impresses that precept on those who are listening as no emphasis or repetition can do.

MUCH WITH GOD, MUCH LIKE GOD.

Such a motto can be illustrated by the story of "that disciple whom Jesus loved," or by the story of Moses on the Mount, and enforced with such passages as, "We shall be like him, for we shall see him as he is," and, "We all, with open face beholding as in a glass the glory of the Lord, are changed into the same image." The following exercises are only suggestive of a multitude of others:

TRUST YE IN THE LORD FOREVER:

FOR IN THE

LORD JEHOVAH

IS EVERLASTING STRENGTH. ISA. xxvi, 4.

"Ingenious little children sometimes tell you how, with a few letters, they can spell a very large word. With three letters I can spell *bereavement.* With three letters I can spell *disappointment.* With three letters I can spell *suffering.* With three letters I can spell *death.* With three letters I can spell *perdition.* S-i-n—SIN. That is the cause of all our trouble now. That is the cause of our trouble for the future."

"SIN" being printed very large, across it, in another color, may be written the words in italics; above it may then be written, "Christ will save us from ——," and on either side, "No —— in heaven."

II. THE TOPIC EXERCISE.

Next to the motto exercise in simplicity comes the topic exercise, which consists in putting the divisions of an address, or the analysis of a lesson, or the prominent points of a story, upon the blackboard, one after another. For example, "Christ's Miracles of Raising the Dead," by Rev. W. B. Wright:

I. JAIRUS' DAUGHTER—from her BED.
II. WIDOW'S SON—from his BIER.
III. LAZARUS—from the TOMB.

This exercise illustrates the increasing wonder of the three miracles on the dead; one raised just after death from her "bed;" another a few hours after death from his "bier," as he was "carried forth;" and a third from the "tomb," where he had "lain four days already."

JESUS OUR DAVID.

The Shepherd Bag.	The Bible.
Five Pebbles.	1 Tim. i, 15; John iii, 16; Isa. liii, 5; 1 Pet. ii, 24; John iii, 36.
The Sling.	The Holy Spirit.

VICTORY THROUGH CHRIST.

B. F. J.

3. Initial Exercise.

Next in natural order comes the Initial Exercise, by which several important words in the lesson beginning with the same letter are united together with that letter. For example:

From Sin to God.

This exercise may be illustrated by the familiar story of Curtius and the chasm at Rome, and other stories of men who have given their lives for country or friends. Another example of this kind:

The Prodigal.

R ashness.
R uin.
R ebellion.
R epentance.
R eform.

L ost, L oves, S ought, S ecured, R estored, R ejoiced over.

4. The Syllable Exercise.

Next in natural order are those exercises in which several words are bound together by a common syllable. For example:

The Pathway of Jesus.

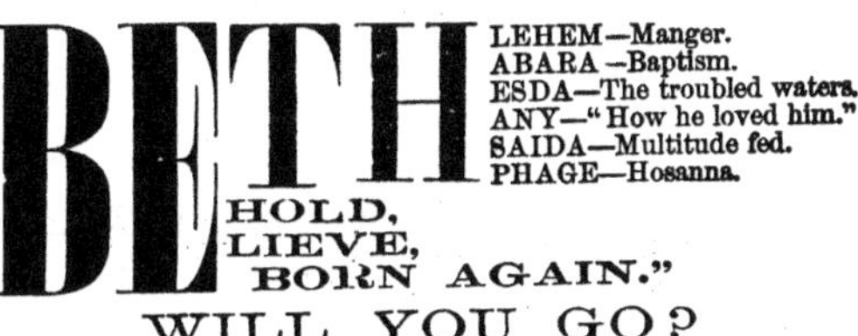

"Behold" Jesus at Bethlehem in the manger—the Prince of heaven wrapped in swaddling-clothes, paying the ransom of your soul; Behold a dove descending and a voice from heaven, at Bethlehem, saying, "This is my beloved Son;" "Behold how he loved him" at Bethany; Behold the cripple saved at Bethesda, the multitude fed at Bethsaida; "Behold thy king cometh (from Bethphage) amid palms and hosannas." Believe in this Christ and you shall be "born again," and have a Christmas and Bethlehem in your own heart; you shall be *baptized* into Christ, raised from the death of sin, fed with angels' food, and your heart filled with "Hosannas." "*Will you go*" in this pathway with Jesus?

5. The Word Exercise.

This class includes exercises, in which two or more passages or statements are bound together by a common word. For example:

WHAT WILL YOU HAVE?—(See Prov. xxiii, 29.)

THEY THAT TARRY LONG AT THE / SEEK MIXED WINE,

The words "What will you—(have)" are not to be written until after all the others have been written and spoken of. Illustrations for this exercise may be taken from the following

"SPECIMENS OF THE WORK DONE INSIDE."

A young man in prison had such a strong thirst for intoxicating liquor that he cut off his hand at the wrist, called for a bowl of brandy in order to stop the bleeding, thrust his wrist into the bowl, and then drank the contents.

A wife was dangerously sick and her husband went for her medicine. On the way home he stopped to drink with a friend; one glass led to others; after a long time he came home stupefied with drink, and threw himself upon the bed where the helpless wife was lying in mortal agony. He woke at midnight, startled by a terrible thunder storm that was raging, and found his wife cold in death at his side.

In a village near Boston, an old man, the slave of appetite, endeavored to get some liquor as a medicine, being unable to get it as a drink. He said he needed it on account of trouble with his feet. Being suspected, he was told he could use it in the drug-store, but could not carry it away. He poured it into his boots, and was seen a few minutes later behind a fence, greedily drinking the liquor from his boots.

Nay, more, a slave of this habit, unable to buy any liquor, stole and drank the spirits with which a corpse had been bathed a few hours before!

6. PHRASE EXERCISE.

This class comprises those exercises in which a common phrase binds together several passages. For example:

ELISHA'S DEFENDERS.—2 *Kings* vi, 16.

"THE LORD OF HOSTS IS
"THEY THAT BE WITH US

ARE MORE THAN THEY
THAT BE
WITH THEM."

"IF GOD BE FOR US
WHO CAN BE AGAINST US?"

When London was shaken with the great earthquake, and houses were falling on every side; when the ground rocked like the sea in a storm, and men cried for mercy, thinking the end of all things had come, Wesley gathered his little band of Christians in their chapel and read calmly to them, as they responded in many a deep and fervent amen, the Forty-sixth Psalm: "God is our refuge and strength, a very present help in trouble. Therefore will not we fear, though the earth be removed," etc.

The expression "*The Lord was with* ——" is associated with Joseph, Moses, Daniel, David, etc. These also may be grouped into a phrase exercise, and the application made to the passage "The Lord of hosts is with us." In the pit where Joseph was cast, the basket-cradle of Moses, the den of lions. and the other places of trial in the lives of those mentioned, God was with them.

7. Table Exercise.

This class comprises those exercises in which several pas sages or thoughts are grouped into some sort of a table For example:

Blessing and Cursing.—Having told the school to find in the Bible, during the previous week, six things that God hates, and eight things that God blesses, hinting, if necessary, that somewhere in Proverbs and Matthew the information may be found, put on the board, before the opening of the school, what is below except the words which follow the figures in each row. These should be drawn from the school by questions, when the blackboard exercise is explained, near the close of the session:

THUS SAITH THE LORD:

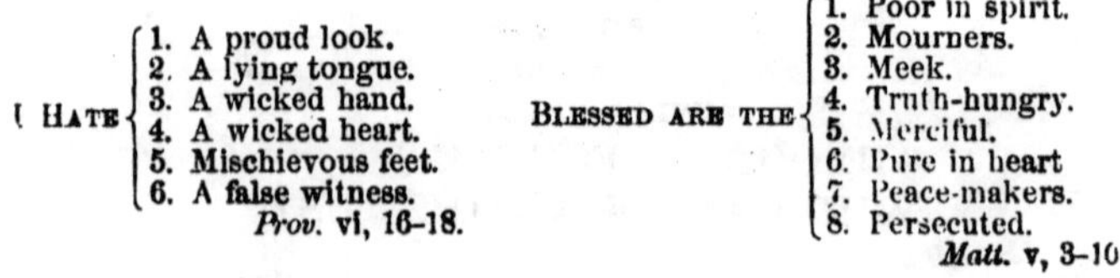

I Hate
1. A proud look.
2. A lying tongue.
3. A wicked hand.
4. A wicked heart.
5. Mischievous feet.
6. A false witness.

Prov. vi, 16-18.

Blessed are the
1. Poor in spirit.
2. Mourners.
3. Meek.
4. Truth-hungry.
5. Merciful.
6. Pure in heart
7. Peace-makers.
8. Persecuted.

Matt. v, 3-10

Below the first group write, "They shall call on the rocks and hills to hide them from the wrath of the Lamb." Under the other, "These are they that follow the Lamb whithersoever he goeth."

The first verses of the First Psalm may be used *above* these groups at the close, giving the *present* condition of things, as the passages below give the *future:*

"BLESSED

Is the man that walketh

NOT	BUT
In the Counsel	His delight is
of the	in the
Ungodly,	Law of the Lord."
(Those things hated.)	(Those things blessed.)

GOSPEL IDEA OF A MAN.

("Add.")
Faith.
Virtue.
Knowledge.
Temperance.
Patience.
Brotherly Kindness.
Charity.

Total—A TRUE MAN.

God is not satisfied with pet virtues; with good temperance men who have no brotherly kindness; with faith in those who have not charity; with virtue, but not according to knowledge. We are to "*add*" these together, having the faith that mounts up on wings as eagles, the virtue that shall run and not be weary, the patience that shall walk and not faint, the brotherly kindness that beareth all things, and the charity that never faileth.

6

8. The Acrostic Exercise.

The acrostic exercise binds several passages or points together by their initial letters being formed into the important word of the lesson or address. For example:

Jesus in the Temple.

OUR Found,
Arguing,
Temple,
How that ye { left us? / sought me?
Engaged, (in Father's business.)
Returned.

The word "Our" and the acrostic letters "Father" in red, and the rest in white.

Watchfulness.

WATCH
YOUR
Words,
Actions,
Thoughts,
Company.
Hearts.

J. H. Watt.

"FOLLOW ME." (Luke ix, 51–62.)

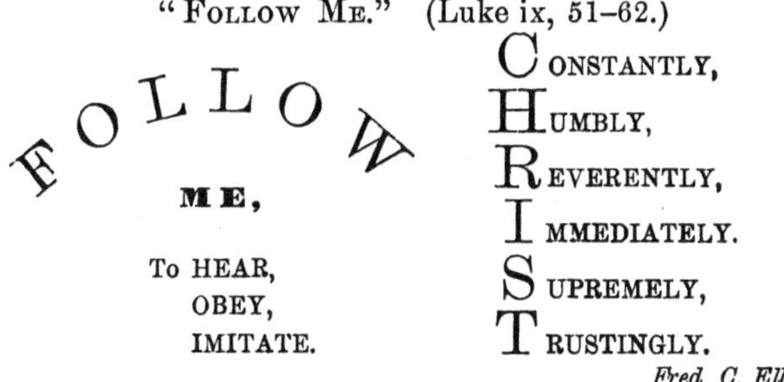

Fred. C. Elliott.

9. PARALLEL AND CONTRAST EXERCISES.

This division includes those exercises where different passages or thoughts are arranged to parallel or contrast with each other to show similarity or antitheses.

It is useful to set before a school "life and death, blessing and cursing," to bring out the contrasts in the life of Christ and in Christian character, etc.

THE TWO TEMPTATIONS.

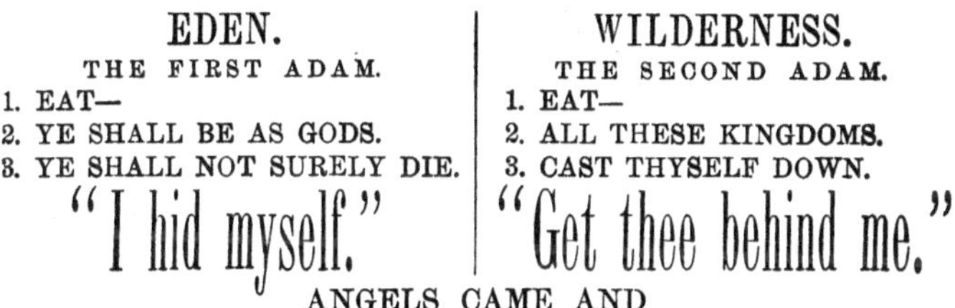

ANGELS CAME AND

DROVE HIM FORTH. | MINISTERED UNTO HIM.

Satan is the same shrewd tempter in the wilderness as in Eden. He first tries *appetite*, then *ambition*, and then *perverts the word of God.* The father of lies said to Adam, "Ye shall be as gods." See him who was to be "as gods" sneaking in the bushes. He said to Christ, "I will give you all the kingdoms of the world," when he did not own enough to rest his foot on. Temptation comes to-day, first to *appetite;* then, for the power of wealth or fame, we are urged to wrong-doing; then we are tempted to "cast ourselves down" into soul-dangers, and even into eternity unprepared, and trust to God's angels. Cancel the three temptations with "*It is written.*"

10. Over-chalking or Canceling Exercise.

Very many impressive exercises may be made by canceling a word or sentence with a better or brighter one. For example:

The Pre-eminence of Jesus, at the Transfiguration.

1. Law—Moses.
2. Prophets—Elias.
3. Gospels—John.
4. Epistles—Peter and James.

Write in some brightly-colored chalk, "Hear ye him" over the first row, after talking about it as it stands; then write "JESUS ONLY" over the other row.

Instead of the books we shall see "Hear ye him;" instead of the men, "Jesus only." As we look upon the mount, Peter and James and John are on their faces; Moses and Elias have faded out in the brightness of Christ's glory, and we "*see no man save Jesus only.*" Below the above exercise print as follows:

LOOK NOT TO
HEAR NOT "WHAT THEY THINK."
DO."
SAY."

Write in red chalk, over the parts opposite "Look," the following, to cancel the error, "to Jesus only." So, after "Hear," the following, "ye him."

First, the exercise standing as it is above, show how we measure and plan by those strange yard-sticks and mirrors "What they *think*" and "What *they do*," and how we always have a hand to the ear for "What *they say.*" Then cancel these errors, and let the revised exercise read, "Look to Jesus only"—"Hear ye him."

THE OIL INCREASED. 2 Kings iv, 1-7.

I. Write on the board the words WIDOW, ELISHA, MIRACLE, as the three points of importance in the lesson. II. Show the condition of the widow. It was of Affliction, Debt, Poverty, Slavery. [As each word is given by the school write it down.] III. What the woman did. She *told* Elisha; *asked* his help; *believed* his word; *obeyed* his command. IV. Next illustrate the process of the miracle. Door was shut; oil was increased; vessels filled; debt paid. V. Now, its spiritual application. The condition of the widow is the condition of ALL. [Either write this word over the word WIDOW, or erase it, and substitute for it.] So, what she did to Elisha, we may do to JESUS. [Substitute *Jesus* for Elisha, or chalk the word over it.] The *miracle* is a type of SALVATION. [Substitute or over-chalk as above.]

The words All, Jesus, Salvation, may be written with large, square chalk, one inch in diameter, or with the flat side of an ordinary crayon. *Rev. J. L. Hurlbut.*

Meaning of the Cross. 1 Cor. i, 23; Acts xviii, 1–11
1 Cor. 1–23.

1. Draw a cross about the center of the board. 2. The three classes of which the lesson speaks. Write in yellow, *Jews;* in blue, *Greeks;* in white, *Believers.* Below, as in the diagram, the word SEEKING. 3. Now, what were the Jews seeking? *A Sign*, [yellow.] The Greeks? *Wisdom*, [blue.] Believers? *Salvation*, [white.] 4. Next write, as in the diagram, FIND. The Jews found in the cross—*Stumbling-block*, [yellow.] The Greeks, etc. 5. Finally, the *result.* Write, in heavy chalk, over one side, *Perish;* on the other, *Saved.* *Rev. J. L. Hurlbut.*

11. The Erasing Exercise.

Similar to the canceling exercise is the erasing exercise, in which the eraser is used to rub out one word, or passage sometimes, in order to substitute another.

Loving Jesus.

George A. Peltz gives a very striking exercise of this class. At first on the board there is this sentence:

"WHY DO I LOVE JESUS?"

After talking a little of this to those who love Jesus he rubs out "Why," and "Do I love Jesus?" is his next point. Then he rubs out "Do" and the interrogation point, and "I love Jesus" stands before the school. Then "I" is rubbed out, and the exhortation "Love Jesus" remains. Then "Love" is erased, and "Jesus" is the only *word* the children see, which suggests the passage, "They saw no man save Jesus only."

How to be Happy This Year.

For New Year's Day the subjoined exercise may be employed. Print on the board—

A NEW YEAR.

Ask the children, "What was the first thing you said this morning?" ("A Happy New Year.") "What did you hear those words with?" ("Ear.") Rub out "Y." Then, "What do you do with the ear?" ("Hear.") Put on "H" before "ear." "Now how shall we make the new year a happy one? If we are not Christians what must we have to be happy?" ("A New Heart.") Add "T," and finish the talk with the words before the eyes of all—

"A NEW HEART.

This is given briefly, by memory, from "The Blackboard."

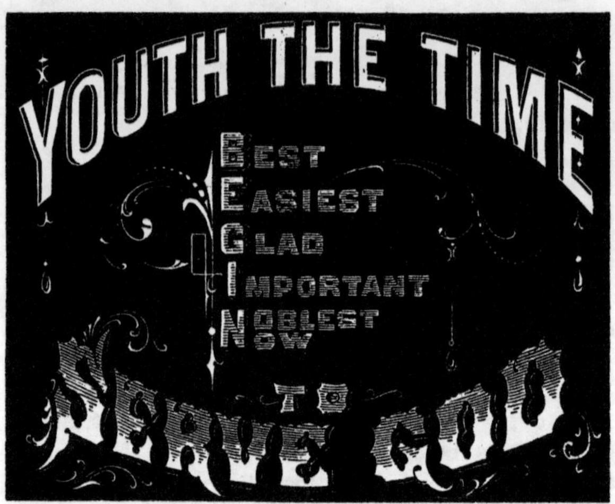

1. Write GOD as the beginning. Next, SERVE GOD. "The TIME." When? YOUTH. 2. Reasons. [Write each word as the reason is announced.] Youth is the *Best* time; develops character. It is the *Easiest* time. It is a *Glad* time; early conversions are happy conversions. *Important*, as the period when habits are formed. *Noblest*, more honorable to give God the bloom of life. 3. Erase all of the column of words except the initials, and show the duty. *Begin to Serve God.* 4. Write at the foot of the column, NOW. The moment when we should begin to serve God.

Rev. J. L. Hurlbut.

The following incident may be used for illustration:

Richard Walter was on his way to school with his slate and books neatly strapped in a bundle, when he felt a hand resting on his shoulder, and turning around he saw a gentleman who said: "I see you have a slate in your bundle; I suppose you have an arithmetic too. What do you cipher in?" "Long division," said Richard. "Will you let me try to work a question in long division on your slate?" the man asked. Richard looked at him in astonishment, and scarcely knew what answer to make. However, Richard thought that he would see what the man would do, and he unbuckled his bundle, and handed slate and pencil to the gentleman. The stranger took them, and, stepping to the side of the path, figured away in silence for a few minutes. By the time he had finished some other boys came along, and stopped to see what was going on. "Good morning, boys," said the gentleman. 'Here's a question in long division I've been trying to work out, and I want you to see if it's right." Richard took the slate, while the boys looked over his shoulder at these figures:

```
29)384,605(12,572
   29
   --
    74
    58
    ---
    166
    145
    ---
     210
     203
     ---
       75
       38
       --
       17
```

"Wrong!" "Wrong!" "It is wrong!" shouted several voices at once. "Where is it wrong?" asked the gentleman. "Why," said Richard, "you made a mistake almost at the very start. Nine from eighteen leaves nine, you've seven." "Is that the only mistake?" said the man. "That is all I see," said Richard. "I guess the rest is all right," said another boy. "Work out the question yourself, and let me see the result," said the gentleman to Richard. When he had done it the gentleman said: "Your quotient is 13,262, and is right. Mine was 12,572, and is wrong; and the boys were all wrong in saying that the only mistake was that made in the beginning, for *as that was wrong every thing that followed it was wrong.* Those figures, though right in themselves, gave me a wrong answer because of **THE ERROR IN THE BEGINNING.**

CHRISTIAN GROWTH.

Mr. C. B. Stout, of New Jersey, makes an excellent address on Christian work and growth on the following plan. He first writes "Go," and speaks of the importance of going somewhere. Then he adds "Right," making "Go Right," and speaks of that. Then he adds "On," which makes "Go Right On," his third point. After developing that thought he writes "Working," and his fourth point is

GO
RIGHT
ON
WORKING.

After emphasizing this he *erases* all except the initials, leaving the exhortation, "GROW."

12. Word-Symbol Exercise.

This class includes all those exercises in which passages of Scripture or other words are shaped into symbols of Bible truth, as crosses, stars, plows, shields, ships, roads, etc. For example:

The Precious Cross.

HE
IS
PRECIOUS
BLOOD
PROMISES
FAITH
TO YOU
THAT
BELIEVE.

See 1 Pet. i, ii; 2 Pet. i. First and last, Christ is "precious" to all that believe. His "blood" is precious, and also the "promises" and "faith" by which we claim and apply it to our hearts. The whole forms the "precious" cross. It would be well to ask on the Sunday previous to the use of this that the scholars should find every thing that Peter calls "precious." Then write only "Precious" on the board before the school, getting the remainder from the scholars. The cross, as it is the most prominent symbol of our holy religion, is often formed in a way similar to that just indicated, in blackboard exercises, as the following examples will show:

Thou
shalt
call
HIS
name
"Believe on the LORD JESUS an l thou shalt be SAVED."
for he
shall
save
HIS
people
from
their
SINS. *J. S. Ostrander.*

I love
them
that
love
"Come unto ME and be saved."
"My son, give ME thine heart."
& they
that
seek
ME
early
shall
find
ME. *Rev'd from I. W. C*

THE YOKE OF CHRIST.

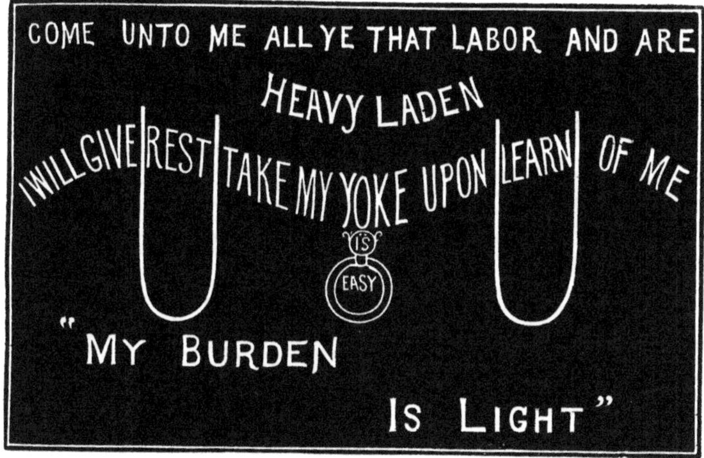

MY YOKE IS EASY. (Matt. xi, 30.)

I place first upon the board the two *U's*. I am about to address *you* and *you*, each of you. I want the ears and eyes of all. We are carrying *burdens*, guilt, sin, weighed down under the wrath of God. We are tired of sin, a burden; we are *heavy laden*. Jesus says, "Come unto me," etc. Will you come? He will tell *you* how to get rid of this load. He will teach *you*. He says, "*Learn of Me.*" How? Why? *You* want *rest*. "*I will give you rest.*" How? "Take *my yoke* upon *you*." How can we get rest by taking another yoke upon us? His yoke *is easy*. *We bear the yoke.* Christ bears our sins, etc. "Cast thy burden on the Lord," or Jesus, often. "Great peace have they that love thy law;" all joy, etc. Burdens light; "These light afflictions," etc. The invitation, "*Come unto ME all ye that labor and,*" etc. The owner brings the yoke, and the oxen come under it. They assist in reaping the fields, and in winter live on the harvest, etc. Sometimes we see one ox lying down and the other standing, *both joined to one yoke*, one ready for work, the other at ease. So Christ waits for the idle Christian. "*Woe unto them that are at ease in Zion.*"—*J. S. Ostrander.*

THE MILESTONES OF THE NARROW WAY.

In the city of Rome distances were measured by milestones that counted in each direction from the golden milestone in the public square. So all along our way God puts up the milestones of the promises, beginning with the Golden Milestone of Conversion.

Make the outline of a road, with milestones, *each formed of the words of a promise.*

13. THE MAP EXERCISE.

This class includes simply geographical outlines and maps on the blackboard. Whenever the geography of a lesson is to be brought out, no means is more useful than a blackboard outline, on which the scholars can direct the blackboard delineator in marking the prominent points.

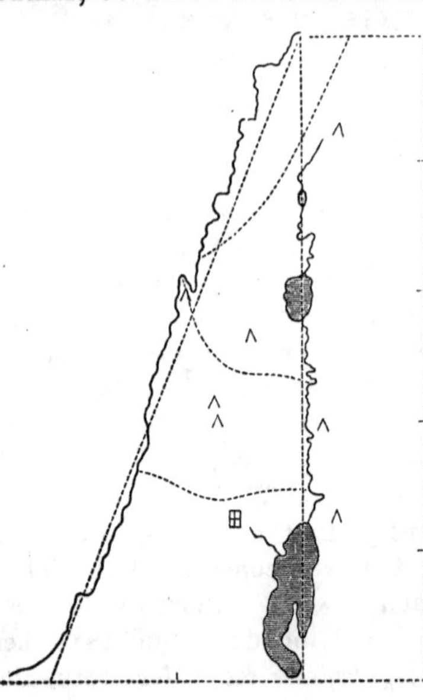

A map whose construction the eye has witnessed will be retained more readily and vividly in the mind than one far more elaborate displayed when complete. The lack of exactness and finish will be more than compensated in the distinctness and impressiveness attained.

The outline here presented will be a convenient form of carrying the shape of Palestine in the memory.

The plan we have just given and described is designed simply to afford the teacher an easy mode of drawing an outline of Palestine; but when one has thus been made, only one or two points in the country, those that are to be connected with the lesson, should be brought out, and no irrelevant parts of the map delineated. We insert two most excellent illustrations of this, which have been contributed to this book by Mrs. Samuel W. Clark. The first is on

SAUL'S CONVERSION.

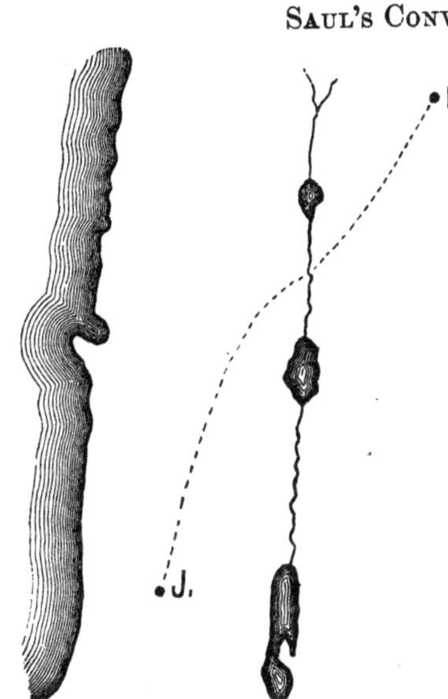

In connection with this journey from J. (Jerusalem) to D. (Damascus) the story of Saul's persecuting spirit, the light, the voice, the blindness with which he entered Damascus, and the other interesting incidents of his conversion, may be described. Some writer has said of this scene that "Christ himself stood as sentry for his little Church at Damascus, and saved it from its bitterest persecutor."

The following Sabbath the map was continued and enlarged to include a part of Paul's first missionary journey.

PAUL, THE FIRST MISSIONARY.

A careful reading of the Scripture narrative (Acts ix–xiii, 13) will give the journey indicated upon this map. A. is Antioch in Syria, S. is Seleucia, Sa. is Salamis, Ph. is Paphos, P. is Perga, A. P. is Antioch in Pisidia, and I. is Iconium,

A study of the history will enable the teacher to tell the story, not in stereotyped phrases, but as an interesting narrative of

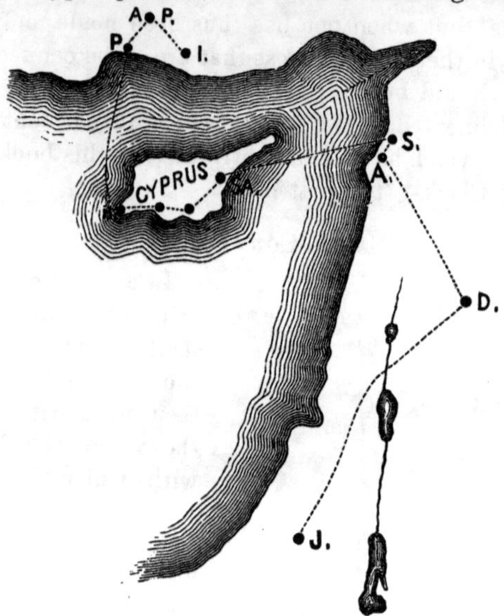

travel. As the history of Paul is continued on following Sabbaths, the new countries may be added and the three journeys kept distinct by three different colors of chalk. Only a little will be added to the map at once, and that thoroughly explained, so that at the close a life-long remembrance of Paul's wanderings will be secured. An interesting exercise may be conducted with this map, such as is suggested on pages 58, 59. The school may be divided into sections, *each of them having one of Paul's journeys*, on which they are to prepare. Then beginning with the map, as on page 130, the line may be increased and the places added, one after another, until all the journeys of Paul are completed, and he has "finished his course." Appropriate selections of Scripture, hymns, recitations, and readings will add to the interest of the exercise. The whole may be named, "From Damascus to Rome."

Dr. M'Cook, in a map which he made upon the blackboard at an institute in Philadelphia, took the Sea of Galilee as a unit of measure, and about one length above it placed Lake Merom; about six lengths below, measuring by the eye simply, the Dead Sea, making a crooked line to connect them, as the Jordan, with small streams branching out from it at appropriate places; about three lengths to the left of the Sea of Galilee he made Mount Carmel, and then slanted the line inward above and outward below, and, after a few additions of mountains and towns connected with the locality he desired to speak of, the map presented a very good representation of Palestine. If a variety of colors are used for water, shore, mountains, towns, rivers, etc., it will add greatly to the clearness and beauty of the map.

If the scholars can be induced to reproduce these maps from memory on their slates at home, and afterward bring them to their teachers, it will fix them yet more clearly in their mind.

Sometimes it is well to make a local map without the outline of the country as its frame-work, as the following for

CHRIST AT JACOB'S WELL.

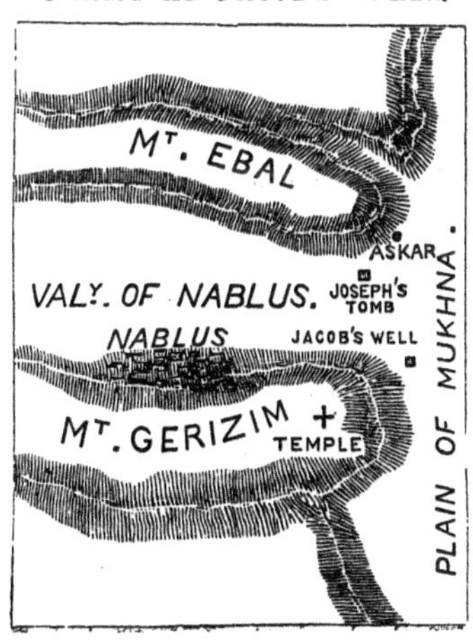

14. The Outline Exercise.

Last and best of all is the outline exercise—outline drawings for the illustration of truth.

Most of the outlines are only the putting into chalk of Bible metaphors and similes. Those of this kind are by far the best, and seldom is it well to represent any other outlines on a Sabbath-school blackboard. We might make one important exception in favor of the religious symbols of the Church, which are given in the Appendix. They offer a wide range for appropriate outline exercises. As a rule, elaborate outlines are not desirable, although a school that has an excellent artist may as properly have a beautiful picture on one side of its blackboard as on its wall. In almost every case the simplest outlines, drawn at the time of explanation, without special effort at ornament or perfection, are the best.

From the Cradle to the Coffin.

Mr. Stout makes a very impressive lesson with a simple line:

C | ———————————————— | C

He tells the schools that the line they see is the picture of every human life from the cradle to the coffin. Every one that hears him is at some point on that line. They all wish that point may be nearer the first "C" than the other, but it may be very near the last, etc. The same excellent speaker makes an impressive exercise for teachers by making two "Cs" as above, and then connecting them by a curve, saying, "The teacher's orbit should be from the closet of prayer to the class;" and then, making another curve from the second "C" back to the first, he adds, "and from the class to the closet."

Another very simple exercise comes to us from the ancients:

"Pythagoras used the letter Y as a symbol of human life. 'Remember,' says he, 'that the foot of the letter represents infancy, and the forked top the two paths of virtue and vice, one or the other of which people are to enter upon after attaining the age of discretion."

Another exercise as simple as that just mentioned is to represent with two lines, meeting at right angles, the coming together of

Philip and the Eunuch.

After the story of their journeys and meeting is told, when the separation is mentioned, continue the lines so that they will form a cross.

The Treasurer of Candace found the cross as Philip "preached unto him Jesus" from the fifty-third of Isaiah. When the Christian is willing to obey the leadings of the Spirit, and the awakened one is desiring to know the way, God's providence will bring them together, and both shall be blessed. "Jesus in the Old Testament," "Drawing near to those we would benefit," "Preaching Jesus to single hearers by the roadside and fireside," and other such topics, may be presented from this story and outline.

The First Love Lost.

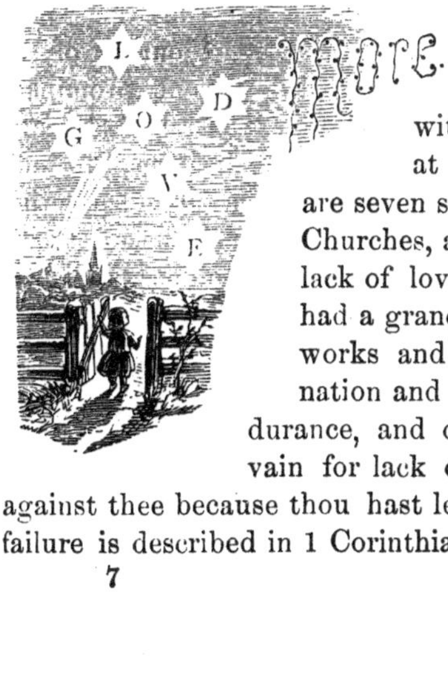

Another simple exercise is the accompanying star cross, that may be used with the letter to the Church at Ephesus in Rev. xi. There are seven stars, the angels of the seven Churches, and one of them is falling for lack of love. The Church at Ephesus had a grand record in some respects—works and labor and patience, indignation and punishment for evil-doers, endurance, and other virtues, but all was in vain for lack of love: "I have somewhat against thee because thou hast left thy first love." A similar failure is described in 1 Corinthians xiii.

THE SEA-PATH. (Exod. xiv, 9, 19–22, 27.)

MOUNTAIN.

EGYPTIANS.____ISRAEL.____SEA.

MOUNTAIN.

Describe the situation of Israel. The enemy behind, mountains on either side, the sea in front. But God opened a path through the sea. Israel went over. The Egyptians were drowned. The Egyptians trusted in their horses and chariots, Israel trusted in God. "*Some trust in chariots,*" etc. Psalm xx, 7.

Use the map not only historically, but also to show that when God bids us "go forward" he always clears our way as we go. "Though we pass through the waters, they shall not come nigh us." "Though a host should encamp against us, in God shall we be confident."

THE WANDERING PATH.

An excellent illustration of the going forward and backward, the faithfulness and faltering of many Christians, may be made by drawing the crooked line of the journey of the Israelites through the wilderness, marking not only prominent places, but also, at proper points, "Manna," "Brazen serpent," "Water from the rock," "Fowls from the heavens," to indicate God's goodness; and such passages as these, at other places, when they begin to turn back, "Much discouraged," "Longing for flesh-pots," "Rebelling," "Golden calf," etc., to represent not only the historical facts, but also our proneness to wander.*

* A concert exercise on this journey, entitled "The Christian Pilgrimage," has been prepared by the author of this book in connection with Dr. Eben Tourjée. The circulars are used both for concert and praise meetings, and are published by Eben Shute, 40 Winter-street, Boston, Mass. Price, $1 50 per hundred.

SATAN AND THE SAVIOUR.

The following exercise is contributed by Rev. J. M. Freeman, and fully explains itself:

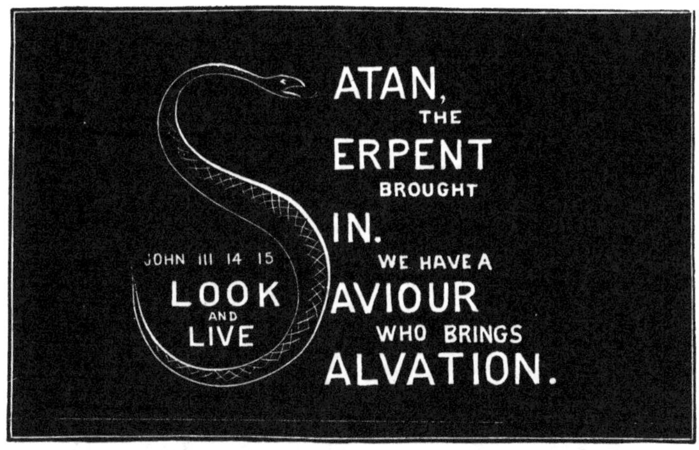

INFANT CLASS BLACKBOARD LESSON: *

Visit of the Wise Men to Bethlehem—Matt. ii, 1–12.

* In using this exercise the teacher can refer to several passages which speak of the Bible as a guide, as, for instance, Psalm cxix, 105; and for the reverse refer to Prov. xxiii, 26, and parallel passages.

(*Reverse.*)

THEIR GIFT.	OUR GIFT.
GOLD, Frankincense, Myrrh.	OUR HEARTS.

—*D. B. H.*

TEMPERANCE EXERCISE.

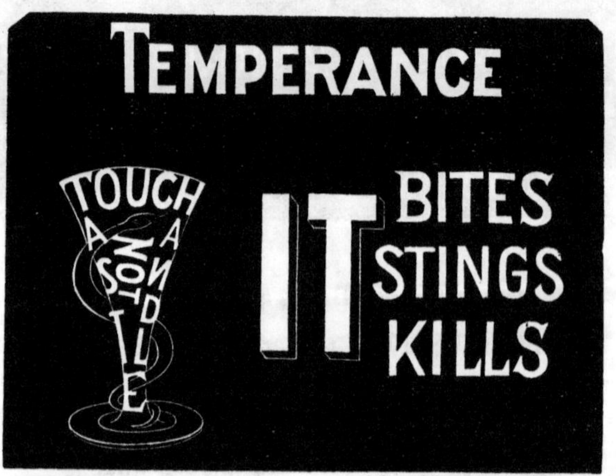

—*Mrs. Samuel W. Clark.*

WATER AND RUM.

Draw a water pitcher and rum bottle, and make on them the following acrostic exercises:

Watchful,
Active,
Truthful,
Excellent,
Rich.

Rascality,
Uncleanness,
Murder.

SATAN'S SPIDER-WEB.*

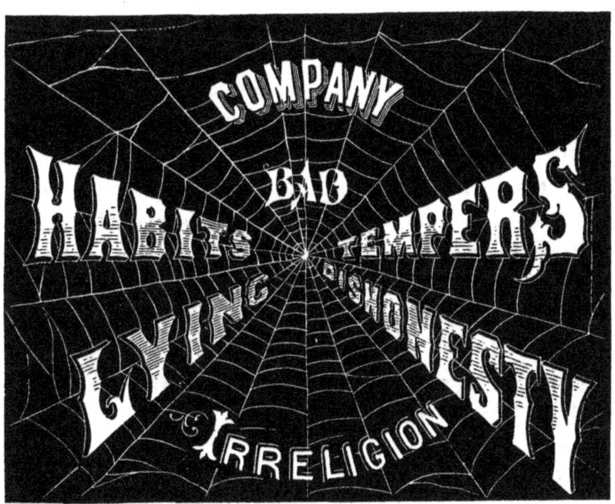

1. Draw in advance the *web*, covering the whole board.

2. Write in each compartment, in order, Bad Company, Bad Habits, Bad Tempers, Lying, Dishonesty, and Irreligion, and as each is written, in presence of the school, show its danger and evil influence. *Rev. J. L. Hurlbut.*

SALVATION OF THE PRODIGAL. Luke xv, 11–32.

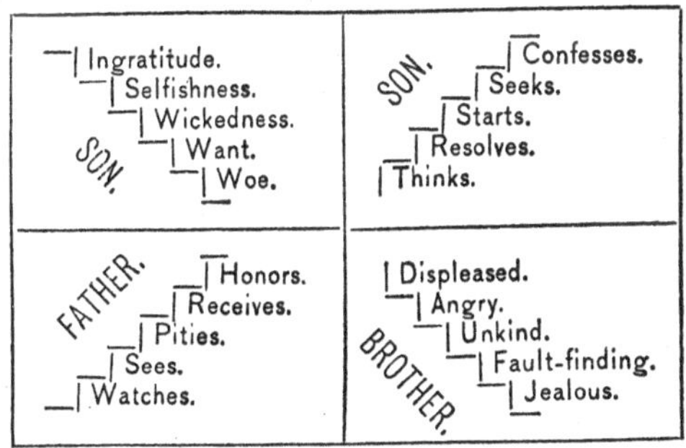

* May be easily adapted to lessons on 1 Kings xii, 25–33; 2 Kings v, 20–27; 2 Kings xvii, 6–18.

1. The steps of the Prodigal away from his Father.
2. The steps of the Son back to the Father.
3. The steps of the Father toward the Son.
4. The steps of the Brother away from his Father.

The prodigal counted on a father's frown and a servant's place, and a life of hard service at his home; but instead of the frown the father cut short his confession with loving embraces, and before he could ask for a servant's place the father called for the ring and best robe; instead of the servants' table he sat down to the fatted calf at the father's side; instead of being hurried into the fields to work they began to be merry with his "welcome home."—*Anonymous.*

The following Normal Class Paper of Rev. Dr. Vincent might be used as a concise outline for discussing, in a teachers' meeting or convention, the whole field of illustration treated in this volume:

The Laws of Illumination.

1. There is great power in the Light.

[It arrests attention. It holds attention. It intensifies attention. It rewards attention.]

2. There is such a thing as putting light into lessons. Lesson illumination is very important.

3 A definition.

Lesson illumination is the employment of those elements in teaching by which the delighted attention of the pupil is attracted toward a lesson, and its instructions rendered more clear to his understanding.

4. Peculiarities of the pupil to be understood in attempting to attract him to a lesson.

   1. The pupil delights in seeing.
   2. The pupil delights in imagining.
   3. The pupil delights in comparing.
   4. The pupil delights in knowing.

5. Means of illumination adapted to the pupil's peculiarities.

   1. The sight.

   Objects, diagrams, maps, pictures, action.

   2. The imagination.

   Word-pictures, stories.

3. Comparisons.

Similes, metaphors, parables, types, symbols, analogies.

4. Knowledge.

History, science, art, travels, Biblical truths.

6. The laws of illumination.

1. The best light to shed on a Bible lesson is Bible light.
   The teacher should therefore make a large use of Bible facts, narratives, parables.
2. To use Bible-light in illuminating a lesson, the teacher should be very familiar with the history, geography, poetry, manners, and customs of Bible times, etc.
3. The teacher should use freely and wisely the facts of every-day life, with which his pupils are most familiar.
4. Illustrations are multiplied by the habit of observation.
5. The teacher should study the masters of illustration in books, in sermons, essays, etc.
6. He should keep scrap-books for the preservation of illustrative material.
7. He should acquire facility in the use of illustration by patient and constant practice.
8. The teacher should use illustrations for the better teaching of the lesson, never to fill up time, to amuse the class, or to display his genius.
9. He should not use too many illustrations.
10. He should, by an apt illustration at the beginning of the lesson, excite the curiosity of his pupils, and thus lead them to self-activity in study.
11. He should remember that the best illustrations are those which come spontaneously while he is endeavoring to make clear to his pupils a truth which is clear to himself.
12. He should remember that in word-picturing the pupil will acquire no more vivid view of the lesson than the teacher himself possesses.
13. He should never unnecessarily use visible and material things to illustrate spiritual truth.
14. He should converse much with children and plain people during the week on the subject of the lesson.
15. To live a godly life is the best way to light up a lesson that a teacher can possibly employ.
16. He should always do the very best in his power, and trust results with the Master whom he serves.

Thus we have spoken of the seven departments of eye teaching. They should ever be as the seven golden candlesticks of Revelation, not attracting the eyes of men to themselves, but only revealing the glory of Him who cried from their midst,

"I AM ALPHA AND OMEGA, THE BEGINNING AND THE ENDING, THE FIRST AND THE LAST."

PATMOS.

www.ingramcontent.com/pod-product-compliance
Lightning Source LLC
LaVergne TN
LVHW011120110826
845150LV00008B/2195

* 9 7 8 1 4 2 5 5 0 6 5 9 9 *